Algernon Charles Swinburne

The Queen-Mother, and Rosamond

Algernon Charles Swinburne

The Queen-Mother, and Rosamond

ISBN/EAN: 9783744689571

Printed in Europe, USA, Canada, Australia, Japan

Cover: Foto ©Thomas Meinert / pixelio.de

More available books at **www.hansebooks.com**

THE QUEEN-MOTHER

AND

ROSAMOND.

THE QUEEN-MOTHER

AND

ROSAMOND.

BY

ALGERNON CHARLES SWINBURNE,

AUTHOR OF "ATALANTA IN CALYDON."
AND "CHASTELARD."

BOSTON:
TICKNOR AND FIELDS.
1866.

SECOND EDITION.

UNIVERSITY PRESS: WELCH, BIGELOW, & CO.,
CAMBRIDGE.

PERSONS REPRESENTED.

CHARLES IX.
HENRY, King of Navarre,
GASPARD DE SAULX, Marshal of Tavannes,
HENRY, Duke of Guise, } *Catholic Nobles.*
PIERRE DE BOURDEILLES, Abbé de Brantôme,
The Admiral COLIGNY,
M. DE LA NOUE,
M. DE TELIGNY,
M. DE LA ROCHEFOUCAULD, } *Huguenot Nobles*
M. DE MARSILLAC,
M. DE SOUBISE,
M. DE PARDAILLAN,
CINO GALLI, Jester to the Queen-Mother.
Two Captains.

CATHERINE DE' MEDICI, Queen-Mother.
MARGARET, Queen of Navarre.
CLAUDE, Duchess of Lorraine.
Duchess of Guise.
DENISE DE MAULÉVRIER,
YOLANDE DE MONTLITARD, } *Maids of Honor.*
ANNE DE SAULX,
RENÉE DE BARBEZIEUX,

*Soldiers, People, Attendants, &c. Scene, Paris,
Time, Aug. 22 – 24, 1572.*

THE QUEEN-MOTHER.

ACT I.

Scene I. *Environs of the Louvre.*

Enter Marsillac, Pardaillan, Soubise, *and others, masked ; the* Duchess *of* Guise, *and other Ladies.*

Marsillac.

NO, not the king, sir, but my lord of Guise ;
I know him by the setting of his neck,
The mask is wried there.

Par.   Are not you the queen ?
By the head's turn you should be ; your hair too
Has just the gold stamp of a crown on it.

Duch. You do dispraise her by your scorn of me.

Par. Not the queen ? then that hair 's real gold of yours
And no white under ?

Sou.   Speak low, sirs ; the king —
See him there, down between the two big stems,
Wearing a rose, some damozel with him
In the queen's colors.

1*

Mar.   Ill colors those to wear;
I doubt some loose half of a Florentine,
Clipt metal too.

Par.   Lower: they are close by this;
Make space, I pray you; Christ, how thick they get!

                       [*The Courtiers fall back.*

       Enter the King *and* DENISE DE MAULEVRIER.

Ch. Why do you pluck your hands away from me?
Have I said evil? does it hurt you so
To let one love you?

Den.   Yea, hurts much, my lord.

Ch. Such soft small hands to hide in mine like birds —
Poor child, she pulls so hard — hush now, Denise,
The wrist will show a bruise, I doubt.

Den.   My wrist?
This is a knight, a man gilt head and feet,   ·
And does such villanous things as that!

Ch.   Yea now,
Will you not weep too? will you cry for it?
So, there, keep quiet; let one loose the mask;
Show me the rivet.

Den.   No, no, not the mask;
I pray you, sir — good love, let be the clasp,
I will not show you — ah!

Ch.   So, so, I said
This was my lady, this one? let the rest
Go chatter like sick flies, the rest of them,

I have my gold-headed sweet bird by the foot
To teach it words and feed it with my mouth.
I would one had some silk to tie you with
Softer than a man's fingers be.
 Den.   I too ;
Your finger pinches like a trap that shuts.
 Ch. Come then, what penance do you think to get
Now I have trapped you ?   No, my sweet Denise,
No crying, no dear tears for it: no, love,
I am not angry.   Why did you break from me ?
 Den. Because I would not have a touch of you
Upon me somewhere ; or a word of yours
To make all music stupid in my ear.
The least kiss ever put upon your lips
Would throw me this side heaven, to live there.   What,
Am I to lose my better place i' the world,
Be stripped out of my girdled maiden's gown
And clad loose for the winter's tooth to hurt,
Because the man 's a king, and I — see now,
There 's no good in me, I have no wit at all ;
I pray you by your mother's eyes, my lord,
Forbear me, let the foolish maiden go
That will not love you ; masterdom of us
Gets no man praise : we are so more than poor,
The dear'st of all our spoil would profit you
Less than mere losing ; so most more than weak
It were but shame for one to smite us, who
Could but weep louder.

Ch.   But Denise, poor sweet,
I mean you hurt, I smite you? by God's head
I 'd give you half my blood to wash your feet.

[*They pass.*

Duch. To speak truth, I 'm a German offset, sir,
And no high woman; I was born in Cleves,
Where half the blood runs thick.

Par.   Ay, with your tongue and head,
Tell me of German! your silk hair, madam,
Was spun in Paris, and your eyes that fill
The velvet slit i' the mask like two fair lamps,
Set to shake spare gold loose about the dark —
Tell me of German!

Duch.   See then in my hands;
You have good skill at palm-reading, my lord?

Par. The glove smells sweet inside; that 's good to
    touch.

Duch. Give me my glove back.

Par.   By your hand, I will not.

Duch. There is no potency of oath in that;
My hands are weak, sir.

Par.   By your eyes then, no.

Duch. I pray you, for your courtesy, sweet lord,
Leave me the glove yet.

Par.   Bid me tear it first ·
I 'll wear this whether iron gird or silk,
Let snatch at it who will; and whoso doth,
I 've a keen tongue ensheathed to answer with.

Duch. I do beseech you, not my glove, fair sir,
For your dear honor, — could you have such heart ?

Par. Yea, truly ; do but see me fasten it ;
Nay, it drops ; help me to set in the wrist.
The queen comes ; I shall cross her sight with this :
If you be woman, as you said, of hers,
It will make sharp the inward of her soul
To see it.

Enter the Queen-Mother, GUISE, *and Attendants ;* CINO GALLI,
and Ladies, masked.

Ca. So, Denise is caught by this ;
Alack, the wolf's paw for the cat's, fair son !
That tall knight with a glove wrought curiously,
Whose friend, think you ?

Gui. Some lady's here, no doubt ;
Not mine, as surely.

Par. Not yours, my lord of Guise.

Ca. Your wife's glove, is it ? sewn with silk throughout,
And some gold work, too : her glove, certainly.

Gui. Take no note of him, madam ; let us go.
[*They pass.*

Par. You Catholics, her glove inside my cap,
Look here, I tread it in the dirt : you, Guise,
I tread a token under foot of mine
You would be glad to wear about the heart.
Here, madam, have it back ; soiled in the seam
Perhaps a little, but good enough to wear
For any Guise I see yet.

Duch.   I keep it for him.

[*Exit* Duchess.

Cino. If he be wise I am no fool.   One of you
Bid him come sup with me.

Par.   What fare, good fool ?

Cino. A sacrament of eye-water and rye-bread
Changed to mere foolish flesh and blood to sup, sir.

﹡ *Yolande.* 'Ware stakes, my Cino; is this a head to
     roast ?
Think, my poor fool's tongue with a nail through it,
Were it no pity ?

Cino.   Fire goes out with rain, child.
I do but think, too, if I were burnt to-morrow,
What a waste of salt would there be ! what a ruin of silk
     stuff !
What sweet things would one have to hear of me,
Being once got penitent !   Suppose you my soul's father,
Here I come weeping, lame in the feet, mine eyes big —
" Yea, my sin merely ! be it not writ against me
How the very Devil in the shape of a cloth-of-gold skirt
Lost me my soul with a mask, a most ungracious one,
A velvet riddle ; and how he set a mark on me,
A red mark, father, here where the halter throttles,   ·
See there, *Yolande* writ broad " ; yet, for all that,
The queen might have worn worse paint, if it please you
     note me,
If her physic-seller had kept hands cleaner, verily.

Yol. Kind Cino ! dost not look to be kissed for this
     now ?

Cino. Be something modest, prithee : it was never good
    time
Since the red ran out of the cheeks into the lips.
You are not patient ; to see how a good man's beard
May be worn out among you !
    Anne.   Virtuous Cino !
    Cino. Tell me the right way from a fool to a woman,
I 'll tell thee why I eat spiced meat on Fridays.
    Yol. As many feet as take the world twice round, sweet,
Ere the fool come to the woman.
    Cino.   I am mocked, verily ;
None of these slippers but have lightened heels.
I 'll sit in a hole of the ground, and eat rank berries.
    Yol. Why, Cino ?
    Cino.   Because I would not have a swine's mouth
And eat sweetmeats as ye do. It is a wonder in heaven
How women so nice-lipped, discreet of palate,
Should be as easy for a thief to kiss
As for a king's son ; like the common grass
That lets in any sun or rain, and wears
All favors the same way ; it is a perfect wonder.
    Yol. A stole for Cino ; pray for me, Fra Cino.
    Cino. Vex me not, woman ; I renounce the works of
    thee.
I 'll give the serpent no meat, not my heel,
To sweeten his tooth on. I marvel how your mother
Died of her apple, seeing her own sense was
So more pernicious ; the man got but lean parings,

And yet they hang too thick for him to swallow.
Well, for some three or four poor sakes of yours,
I 'll eat no honey.

Anne.　　　　Wherefore no honey, Cino ?
One saint ate honey before your head had eyes in it.

Cino. I would not think of kissing, and it remembers
　　me.
Here are two scraps of Venus' nibbled meat ;
Keep out of the dish, as ye respect me, children,
Let not love broil you on a gold spit for Sundays.

　　　　　　　　　　　　　　[*They retire.*

　　　　　　Re-enter the King *and* DENISE.

Ch. Nay, as you will then.

Den.　　　　　　　　Not for love indeed,
Not for love only, but your own fair name,
The costliness and very price of it,
I am bold to talk thus with you.　The queen, suspicious
And tempered full of seasonable fears,
Does partly work me into this ; truth is it,
There 's no such holy secret but she knows
As deep therein as any ; all changes, hopes,
Wherewith the seed-time of this year goes heavy,
She holds and governs ; and me, as all my fellows,
Has she fed up with shreds and relics thrown
From the full service and the board of time
Where she sits guest, and sees the feast borne through ;
I have heard her say, with a sigh shaking her,
There 's none more bound to pray for you than she,

And her you love not; and how sore it seems
To see the poisons mingle in your mouth,
And not to stay them.

  Ch.   Will she say that indeed?
Denise, I think if she be wise and kindly,
And mixed of mother's very milk and love,
She would not say so.

  Den.   I have a fear in me
She doubts your timely speed and spur of blood;
She thinks, being young, you shall but tax her care
And liberal grace with practice and weak tricks;
As thus, say, you conceive of me, fair lord,
As one set on and haled by golden will
(Such lust of hire as many souls hath burnt
Who wear no heat outside) to do you wrong,
To scourge and sting your lesser times with speech,
Trailing you over by some tender lies
On the queen's party; which God doth well believe
To lie as far from me as snow from sun,
Or hence to the round sea.

  Ch.   There 's no trick meant me?

  Den. I pray, sir, think if I, so poor in wit
The times rebuke me, and myself could chide
With mine own heaviness of head, be fit
To carry such a plot and spill none over
To show the water's color I bear with me?
All I lay care to is but talk of love,
And put love from me I am emptier

B

Than vessels broken in the use ; I am sorry
That where I would fain show some good, work somehow
To suit with reason, I am thrown out merely
And prove no help ; all other women's praise
Makes part up of my blame, and things of least account
In them are all my praises. God help some !
If women so much loving were kept wise,
It were a world to live in.

  Ch.   Poor Denise,
She loves not then so wisely ? yea, sweet thing ?

  Den. Did I say that ? nay, by God's light, my lord,
It was ill jested — was not — verily,
I see not whether I spake truth or no.

  Ch. Ay, you play both sides on me ?

  Den.   It may prove so.
I am an ill player, for truly between times
It turns my heart sick.

  Ch.   Fear when one plays false, then.

  Den. As good play false when I make play so hardly.
My hand is hurt, sir; I 'll no more with you.

  Ch. Will you so cheat me ?

  Den.   Even so ; God quit you, sir !
But pardon me ; and yet no pardon, for
I 'll have no stay to find it : were pardon at my feet,
I would not bow to gather it. Farewell.

             [*Exit* DENISE.

  Ch. Even so ? but I 'll have reason ; eh, sweet mouth ?
But I 'll have reason of her, my Denise ;

How such can love one ! all that pains to talk !
What way ran out that rhyme I spun for her ?
To do just good to me, that talk ! sweet pains.
Yea, thus it fell : *Dieu dit* — yea, so it fell.

    Dieu dit ; Choisis ; tu dois mourir ;
    Le monde vaut bien une femme.
    L'amour passe et fait bien souffrir.
    C'est ce que Dieu me dit, madame.
    Moi, je dis à Dieu ; Je ne veux,
    Mon Dieu, que l'avoir dans ma couche,
    La baiser dans ses beaux cheveux,
    La baiser dans sa belle bouche.   [*Exit the* King.

Yol. Now, Cino ?

Cino.   I am considering of that apple still ;
It hangs in the mouth yet sorely ; I would fain know too
Why nettles are not good to eat raw. Come, children,
Come, my sweet scraps ; come, painted pieces ; come.

Anne. On after him ; he is lean of speech and moody ;
Cunning for ill words at such winter-seasons
That come i' the snow like bitter berries. On.
                                  [*Exeunt.*

SCENE II. *In the Louvre.*

Enter King HENRY *and* MARGARET.

Mar. Yea, let him say his will.

Hen.   I will not bear him.
This temperance grows half shame.

Mar.   I doubt God hath

Fashioned our brother of like earth and fire
As moulds you up; be patient; bear with him
Some inches past your humor's mark.

Hen.   Bear what?
By God I will have reason: tell me not;
I love you with the soundest nerve i' the heart,
The cleanest part of blood in it; but him
Even to the sharpest edge and tooth of hate
That blood doth war upon.

Mar.   Keep in this chafe;
Put me in counsel with you.

Hen.   It is no matter.

Mar. I never saw yet how you love and hate.
Are you turned bitter to me? all old words
Buried past reach for grief to feed upon
As on dead friends? nay, but if this be, too,
Stand you my friend; there is no crown i' the world
So good as patience; neither is any peace
That God puts in our lips to drink as wine,
More honey-pure, more worthy love's own praise,
Than that sweet-souled endurance which makes clean
The iron hands of anger.   A man being smitten
That washes his abuséd cheek with blood
Purges it nothing, gets no good at all,
But is twice punished, and his insult wears
A double color; for where but one red was
Another blots it over.   Such mere heat
I' the brain and hand, even for a little stain,

A summer insolence and waspish wound,
Hurts honor to the heart, and makes that rent
That none so gracious medicine made of earth
Can heal and shut like patience. The gentle God
That made us out of pain endurable
And childbirth comforts, willed but mark therein
How life, being perfect, should keep even hand
Between a suffering and a flattered sense,
Not fail for either.

Hen. You do think sweetly of him ;
But on this matter I could preach you out.
For see, God made us weak and marred with shame
Our mixed conception, to this end that we
Should wear remembrance each alike, and carry
Strait equal raiment of humility ;
Not bare base cheeks for wrong to spit across,
Nor vex his print in us with such foul colors
As would make bondsmen blush.

Mar. Let him slip wrong,
So you do reason ; if such a half-king'd man
Turn gross or wag lewd lips at you, for that
Must anger strike us fool ? 'T is not the stamp,
The purity and record of true blood,
That makes Christ fair, but piteous humbleness,
Wherein God witnesses for him, no prince
Except a peasant and so poor a man
God gives him painful bread, and for all wine
Doth feed him on sharp salt of simple tears
And bitter fast of blood.

Hen.   Yea, well ; yea, well ;
And I am patient with you Catholics ;
But this was God's sweet son, nothing like me,
Who have to get my right and wear it through
Unhelped of justice ; all do me wrong but I,
And right I 'll make me.

Mar.   But all this wording-time
I am not perfect where this wrong began ;
Last night it had no formal face to show,
That 's now full-featured.

Hen.   Ah ! no matter, sweet ;
Nothing, pure naught.

Mar.   Have you no shame then current
To pay this anger ?   Nay, as you are my lord,
I 'll pluck it out by the lips.

Hen.   A breath, a threat,
A gesture, garment pulled this way ; nothing.

Mar. You do me wrong, sir, wrong.

Hen.   Well, thus then it fell out ;
By God, though, when I turn to think on it,
Shame takes me by the throat again ; well, thus.
King Charles, being red up to the eyes with wine,
In the queen's garden, meeting me — as chance
Took me to walk six paces with some girl,
Some damozel the queen's choice dwells upon,
Strayed somehow from the broader presence —

Mar.   Well —

Hen. I swear to you by faith and faith's pure lip

That I know — that I did not hear her name
Save of his mouth.

Mar.   I did not ask her name.

Hen. Nor do I well remember it ; forgive,
I think it was not —

Mar.   Pass.

Hen.   Alys de Saulx —

Mar. Marshal Tavannes has no such name akin.

Hen. There 's Anne de Saulx wears longest hair of all ;
A maid with gray grave eyes, — a right fair thing ;
Not she, I doubt me.

Mar.   Worse for you, my lord.

Hen. Ay, worse.   Diane de Villequier is tall —

Mar. Are we at riddles ? — Agnès de Bacqueville ?

Hen. Some such name, surely ; either Châteauroux —

Mar. Her name ? as I am wedded woman, sir,
I know you have it hidden in your mouth
Like sugar ; tell me ; take it on the lip.

Hen. There was a D in it that kissed an M.

Mar. Denise ? a white long woman with thick hair,
Gold, where the sun comes ?

Hen.   Ay, to the ends clean gold.

Mar. Yea, not the lightest thing she has, that hair.

Hen. You hold for true —

Mar.   We have time to come for her.
Keep in your story.

Hen.   Naught, mere naught to tell :
This just ; the king comes, pulls her hand from mine —

Mar. Ah! no more shame?

Hen.   No more in him than that;
Plucked her as hard —

Mar.   As she was glad to go.

Hen. Not so; she trembled to the feet, went white,
Spoke hardly —

Mar.   Kept one hand of them your way?

Hen. Charles caught her wrist up, muttered next her
    ear,
Bade me leave care —

Mar.   Nay, here's more fool than we.

Enter CINO.

Cino. The world was a wise man when he lived by bread
    only;
There be sweet tricks now. How does my worthy sister?

Mar. Not so much ill as to cease thanks for it.
How does thy cap, fool?

Cino.   Warm, I thank it, warm;
I need not wear it patched as much as faith.
I am fallen sick of heavy head; sad, sad;
I am as sick as Lent.

Mar.   Dull, dull as dust;
Thou hadst some nerve i' the tongue.

Cino.   Why, I am old;
This white fool three days older in my beard
Than is your wedding. But be not you cast down;
For the mere sting is honorable in wedlock,
And the gall salve: therefore I say, praise God.

Hen. We do not catch thy sense.

Cino. Let my sense be ;
I say I could weep off mine eye-cases,
But for pity of some ladies who would run mad then.
Do not you meddle.

Mar. What wisdom mak'st thou here ?

Cino. Why, a fool's wisdom, to change wit with blocks.
You were late railing; were she that you did gibe
Clean as her mother made, I tell you verily
The whitest point on you were grime and soil
To her fair footsole.

Mar. Ay, but she 's none such.

Cino. I care not what she be ; do you not gibe,
I care no whit. Let her take twelve or six,
And waste the wicked'st part of time on them,
She doth outstand you by ten elbow-lengths.

Hen. Hath love not played the knave with this fool's
eyes ?

Cino. Let that lie shut, and put you thumb to lip;
For kings are bone and blood ; put flesh to that,
You have the rind and raiment of a man.
If you be wise, stay wise, even for my sake ;
Learn to lie smooth, be piteous and abashed,
And though dirt fall upon your faith and you
Keep your ear sober, chide not with its news,
And use endurance well; so shall he thrive,
That being a king doth crouch, and free doth wive.
Farewell, fair king. [*Exit* CINO.

2

Hen.   This fool is wried with wine.

Mar. French air hath nipped his brains; what ailed
   my mother
To have him north?

Hen.   You bring her in my mind;
Have you no service on the queen to-day?

Mar. I think she would lie privately; she said
She was not well.

Hen.   I pray you then with me.

Mar. I will not with my lord of Pardaillan;
You shall not break me with the king.

Hen.   Men say
Guise hath some angry matter made with him
That I would learn.

Mar.   I am with you by the way;
I have some tricks to tell you of Denise.   [*Exeunt.*

SCENE III.   *A Cabinet.*

The Queen-Mother; DENISE *dressing her hair;* TAVANNES.

Den. Disait amour, voyant rire madame,
   Qui me baisait dessous mes yeux un jour;
   La rose est plus que fleur et moins que femme,
      Disait amour.
   Disait amour; m'est peine éclose en âme;
   Dieu veuille, hélas! qu'elle me baise un jour.
   Ayez merci, car je souffre, madame,
      Disait amour.

Ca. Set the gold higher.   So, my lord Tavannes,
You have no answer of the king ?
 Tav.   Not I ;
The Devil would give over such hard work,
I doubt, as you put me to.
 Ca.   Ah well, well,
I thank you for it.   Tie the next more loose,
You prick my forehead through the hair, Denise.
Strange, my lord marshal, I show less gray spots
Than gold thread in it, surely.   Five years hence,
These girls will put a speckled silver on,
Because the queen's hair turns to dust-color.
Eh, will not you, Denise ?
 Den.   If I wear white,
Gold must be out of purchase ; I 'll get gold
Or wear my head shorn flat, and vex no combs.
 Ca. You put sweet powders in your own too much ;
There, stoop down — you may kiss me if you will —
I smell the spice and orris-root in it.
Fie, this will cheat your face, my poor Denise ;
This will bleach out the colors of your blood,
And leave the hair half old.   See you, lord marshal,
This girl's was never soft and thick like mine :
Mine was so good to feel once, I know well
Kings would have spent their lips in kissing it.
 Tav. I have poor judgment of girls' hair and cheeks ;·
Most women doubtless have some gold and red
Somewhere to handle, and for less or more
I care not greatly.

Ca.   Yea, I do well think once
I had such eyes as time did sleep in them,
And age forbear the purple at their lids ;
And my mouth's curve has been a gracious thing
For kisses to fall near : none will say now
That this was once. I may remember me
That Scotswoman did fleer at my gray face ;
I marvel now what sort of hair she has.

Den. The Queen of Scots lived gently in repute ;
She has much wrong.

Ca.   Put not your judgment to 't ;
The peril that enrings her place about
Is her own whetting. I do something praise,
Yet hardly from the outside of my heart,
Our sister England ; were I set like her,
I might look so.

Tav.   Yea so ? mere heretic ?

Ca. Beseech you, pardon me ; I am all shame
That I so far misuse your holiness.
I know as you are sharp in continence
So are you hard in faith. Mark this, Denise,
These swording-men are holier things than we ;
These would put no kiss on, these would not praise
A girl's hair —

Tav.   Madam, do you jape at me ?

· *Ca.* Scarce let the wine turn in their veins to blood ;
Strangle the knowledge and the note of sense,
Deny that worth ; these eat no grosser meat

Than the cleanest water we dip fingers in ;
Endure beyond the very touch of man,
Have none so soft use of the lip as makes it
Affect the natural way.   Sir, is this true ?

  Tav. Why, if men said you had more teeth than hairs
They would just lie ; and if they call me that
They lie a something harder.

  Ca. ˙   Fie, my lord !
Your good wit to a woman's ? will you say
The dog licks where it bit you, if I say
Forgive, Sir Gaspard, and be friends with me ?
Come, if I make you sit by me, fair knight,
And say the king had never half the wit
To choose you for his marshal ?   Ten years back,
And may be clap some other tens on that,
I mind me well, sir, how you came up here
To serve at Paris ; we had a right king then,
King Francis, with his close black beard and eyes
Near half as royal as your own, I think.
A fair page were you, and had yellow hair
That was all burnt since into brown ; your cheek
Had felt no weather pinch it or sun bite,
It was so red then : but you fought well, sir,
Always fought well ; it was good game to see
Your hand that swung round, getting weight to throw,
Feeling for room to strike ; Gaspard, by God
I would have paid gold coin to turn a man
And get me bone to handle the good steel

And nerves to fight with ; but I doubt me, soon
I should have had the dust to roll into,
Though I were made six men to fight with you.
Yet my arm ached for want of spears to smite —
Eh ? when you ran down that Montgommery
That slew my lord with his side-prick i' the eye ?
Yea surely ; you were my best knight, De Saulx.

    Tav. Madam —

    Ca.   Nay, Gaspard, when I lie of you
Then let your bit rasp at the mouth of me ;
I speak poor truth ; why, this Denise of mine
Would give time up and turn her gold hair gray
To have seen out the season we two saw.

    Den. I would not; (*aside to Cath.*) my lord marshal is
        too lean
To be a fair man.

    Ca.   So, your glove for his ?
We shall have larger passages of war
Except I look to it. Pray you, Denise,
Fetch me my glove, — my spice-box, — anything ;
I will not trust you with my lord ; make in. [*Exit* DENISE.
How like you her ?

    Tav.   A costly piece of white ;
Such perfumed heads can bear no weight inside
I think, with all that waste of gold to bear
Plaited each way ; their roots do choke the brain.

    Ca. There your sense errs ; though she be tender-made,
Yet is there so much heart in her as could

Wear danger out of patience. It is my son I fear
Much more than I doubt her: the king my son
Flutters not overmuch his female times
With love enough to hurt, but turns and takes,
Wears and lets go; yet if she springe him once,
Click, quoth the gin; and there we trap him. See,
This medicine I make out for him is sweet,
More soft to handle than a poppy's bud,
And pleasant as a scented mouth to kiss.

   Tav. Yea, I do see.

   Ca.   Now at this turn of time
He is not perfect; and I have a mean
To bring him to our use. My lord of Guise —

   Tav. Doth he make part of it?

   Ca.   Fear you not him;
He is the blazon patched upon our cloth
To keep the pattern's gold. For the king's self,
I have half possessed him of the deeds to be,
And he hath nothing blenched.

   Tav.   But, to this girl —
What way serves her in this?

   Ca.   Being ignorant,
She does the better work; for her own sake
Trails him my way, assures herself the king
Would pluck the reddest secret from his heart
To show her, as you take the reddest rose
To smell at, if the color go by scent;
That 's all her certainty. What foot is there?

Tav. The king, and hastily.

Ca.   Keep you by me ;
I know his cause.   Let him come in. ·

Enter the King.

Ch.   Fair mother,
Good morrow come upon your majesty.

Ca. The morrow grows upon good night, fair son ;
That will salute me soon with sleep ; you see
I keep not well.

Ch.   Ah, pale by God though, pale !
I 'm sorry — sir, good morrow — hurt at heart.
Hear you my news ?   The admiral is hurt,
Touched in the side — I lie now, not the side,
But his arm hurt — I know not verily,
But he is some way wounded.

Ca.   I am sorry
No goodness walks more clear.   Sir, think you not
That for a color — say a color, now —

Ch. I doubt you do not mean to visit him ?

Ca. But I do mean ; and if your leave hold out
We 'll bid the Guise with us.

Ch.   Have your best way :
Write me content thereof.

Ca.   I thank you, sir.
Lord marshal, you shall pray the Guise for us.

Tav. Madam, I shall ; God keep your grace's health.

                                        [*Exeunt.*

SCENE IV. *The Admiral's House.*

Enter COLIGNY *and* LA ROCHEFOUCAULD.

La R. How do you yet, sir ?

Co.   Ill, yea, very ill :
This snake has pricked me to the heart, to the quick,
To the keenest of it; I believe heartily
I shall not live to foil them.   God mend some !
For live or die, and wounded flesh or whole,
There will be hard things done ; we shall not see
Much more fair time.

La R.   Take better thoughts to you ;
The king is steady; and the Guise wears eyes
Of such green anger and suspicious light
As cows his followers ; even the queen-mother
Walks slower than her wont, with mouth drawn up,
And pinches whiter her thin face ; Tavannes
Goes chewing either lip's hair with his teeth,
Churning his bearded spite, and wears the red
Set on his cheek more steady ; the whole court·
Flutters like birds before the rain begin ;
Salcède, who hates no place in hell so much
As he loathes Guise, lets out his spleen at him
And wags his head more than its use was ; yea,
The main set draws our way now the steel bit
Keeps hard inside their mouths : yea, they pull straight.

Co. You lay too much upon them.

La R.   Not a whit over :

2*   c

They are good men our side ; no dog laps i' the trough
So deep as we do; the best men we have
That France has for us, the best mouths for a hunt,
To wind the quarry furthest ; then to these
A clean cause, friends with iron on the hand,
The king to head, no less.

    Co.   The king, no less ?
Yea, there 's a dog gives tongue, and tongue enough,
Too hot I doubt, too hot ; strikes by the scent.

    La R. Will you think so ? why, there be dog-leashes ;
Pluck hard, you hold him.   Come, I note you though ;
None sticks in your throat but Venus the old brach.

    Co. True, there she sticks, sir ; for your burden saith —
    "Brach's feet and witch's nose
    Breathe which way the quarry blows."

    La R. She 's old, sir, old ; the teeth drop, the smell
    wears ;
No breath in her by this.

    Co.   Enough to breathe
The best of you that snuff about and yelp.
Who stops there in the street ? look out.

    La R.   The king !
So, get you ready ; Catherine here and all,
God save my wits a taking ! here you have them.

    Enter the King, Queen-Mother, GUISE, *and Attendants.*

    Ch. Do not rise up, sir ; pray you keep your place ;
Nay now, by God's face, look, the cloak slips off;
Nay, be more patient.

Co.   Dear and gracious lord,
If you be pleased to look on my disease
As not my will, but a constraint to me
Less native than my garments, I have hope
You may forgive it.
Ch.   Yea, we do, we do.
Ca. It was not, sir, your sickness we took pains
To come and visit; what's no friend of yours
Is even as our own felt infirmity,
And should be held so.
Ch.   True, sir, by God it should.
Ca. We therefore pray you have no care of that,
But as we do, respect it.
Ch.   Do not, sir.
Co. Madam, a sick man has not breath or tongue
To answer salutation of such worth ;
But even the very blood that pain makes war on
*Is healed and sound by this.   From stronger heart
Than ere I saw you was in me, now touched
And comforted by favor, I pay thanks
The best I have ; and none so poor man pays
A rent of words more costly.
Ca.   My fair lord,
This compliment has relish of more health
Than was believed in you ; I am most glad
That footless rumor which makes wing to go
Reports you something lesser than you seem ;
So making keener with new spice to it

Our very edge of pleasure, the fine taste
That waits on sudden sweetness. Sir, nathless,
No compliment it was we came to beg,
No alms of language and frayed garb o' the court
That makes no wear for men; but to do grace indeed
Rather to us than you, whose worth no friend
Can top with favor.

  Co.   It shows the more love in you.

  Ca. Also, my lord, for such poor part as mine,
I pray you be not jealous to receive
Assurance of me with how sore a hurt
Ill news of you made passage most unkind
Into my knowledge ; and with how dear a price
I would have bought a chance to succor you
Whose wound was sickness to me. So God love my son,
As I have put my prayer for your good hap
Between two tears before him ; yea, never shall he
Get worship of me but I'll speak of you
As the leader of my loves, the captain friend
Among my nearest. Sir, the king knows well
How I speak of you ; see now, let him say
Whether I lie or no in loving you.

  Ch. Ay, sir, there 's no such day or night-season
But she holds to you, none but the admiral,
That good lord, that best counsellor, strong ward
For any king to hang by ; time has been, sir,
I have turned sick of hearing your grave name
So paddled over, handled so ; my lord,

There's no man, none in the world, my mother mates with
    you
Save two, that's I and God.
    Gui.   And that's a courtesy.
    Co. My lord of Guise, I saw you not; this day,
As men do shut the edges of a wound,
Shuts the loud lips of our contention; sir,
This grace you do me shall keep fast my thanks
To your name always.
    Gui.   It is the king's good will
I should be made the servant to his act;
And what grace pleases him to bring me to
I take as title to me; this not least,
To call my poor name a friend's name of yours.
    Co. That makes mine honor.
    Ch.   It was this we came
To see made well up from the Guise to you;
My thought was ever there, yea, nailed to it,
Fastened upon it; it was my meat and sleep,
Prayer at feast-season and my fast at noon,
To get this over.
    Co.   It is well set now.
This hand is hurt I lay into your hand,
But the love whole and the good will as sound
As shall the peace be for us.
    Gui.   I take it so;
Maimed be that hand which first shall loosen it,
Even beyond healing.

Co.   Pardon, my fair lord,
I am but old, you strain my wrist too much.
    Ch. Nay, you are worse hurt than they told us, then;
I pray you show me but the coat, I would
Fain see the coat where blood must stick of yours.
    Co. Sir, there it is.
    Ch.   Ay, no more red than this?
I thank you; was it this way the slit came?
Yea, so, I see; yea, sideways in the sleeve.   ·
Is that the admiral's blood indeed?   Methinks,
Being issued from so famous veins as yours,
This should be redder.   See, well above the wrist;
See, madam; yea, meseems I smell the stain.
    Ca. It is an ill sight.
    Co.   I would give better, sir,
Spill the red residue some worthier way,
If you would heed me.   Trust not each in all,
Nor sew your faith too thinly to men's sleeves;
There is a poisonous faith that eats right out
The sober and sweet heart of clean allegiance,
Leaving for witness of all royalty
Merely the baser flesh; beware of that.
    Ch. I will. — Is not this like men's blood? — I will.
Most like a common fool's; see you, lord Guise,
Here's a great soldier has no blood more worth
Than yours or mine.   By God, how strange is that,
It makes me marvel.   Is your wound near well?
Tush! no more hurt than shall a month see out.

Ca. You have poor sense of sickness ; I fear much
Our friend shall hardly feed on the larger air
This two months hence.   You must keep close, dear lord,
Hide from the insolent and eager time ;
And we not wrong you by the overstay   ⁂
Of foolish friendship, thankworthy in this,
That it knows when to cease, what limit made
To measure its observance by.   Farewell ;
⁂ Think not worse of us that we trouble you,
But know we love you even too well to buy
Our further speech with danger of your hurt,
And had we sounder witness of our love
Would better prove it.   Sir, God keep you well
And give us joy to see you.

Ch.   Farewell, dear father ;
Doubt not but we will lay a present hand
On one that hath so stricken us in you,
And he shall find us sharp.   In trust of that
Keep some thought of this poorest friend you have,
As we of you shall.   Trouble not yourself.
Nay, have your cloak on ; so ; God give you help.
Come with me, my lord Guise ; fair sir, good night.
Yea, night it is now ; God send you good time of it.

               [*Exeunt* King, Queen-Mother, GUISE, &*c.*

    Co.   Good thanks, sir, and farewell. — So: gone, I
    think ?

    La R.   Fair words go with them ! you have good time
    indeed ;

What holidays of honey have they kept,
What a gold season of sentences to warm by,
Even past all summer! a sweet oil-season,
Kept ripe with periods of late wine to finish it!

Co. Ay, the taste of them makes a bitter lip, sir.

La R. Nay, mere feast-honey; did you mark the Guise
once,
How his chin twisted and got rough with smiles,
Like a new cloth rained on? How the nose was wried of
him,
What widow's cheeks he had, never well dried yet?
The sweet speech clung in his throat like a kernel swal-
lowed
In sucking cherries.

Co.   You are too loud yet, too splenetive.

La R. Tush! they are well gone, no fear of them; but
verily
I doubt you saw not how like a dog's his face was,
A dog's you catch with meat in his teeth; by Christ,
I thought he would have cried or cursed outright,
His mouth so wrought.

Co.   Yea, either had done well.

La R. A dog that snarls and shivers with back down,
With fearful slaver about his mouth; "weh, weh,
For God's sake do not beat me, sirs!" eh, Guise?—
With timid foam between his teeth; poor beast, too,
I could be sorry for him.

Co.   Be wise in time, sir,

And save your tears ; this Guise has scope to mend,
Get past these matters; I not doubt the queen
Touches them with a finger-point of hers.

  La R. The queen gets kind ; she lessens and goes out ;
No woman holds a snake at breast so long,
But it must push its head between the plaits
And show across her throat's gold work. Fair sir,
Cure but your doubt, your blood is whole again
And pain washed out at once ; it is the fret of that
Which fevers you so far.

  Co.   This is not so.
I pray you mark : their fires are lit next room,
The smoke bites in our eyelids, air turns weak
And body trembles and breath sickens here.
Sir, I do know this danger to the heart,
To the shape and bone of it, the mouth and eyes,
The place and time, season and consequence ;
By God's head, sir, now, this mere now, this day,
The peril ripens like a wound o' the flesh
That gathers poison ; and we sleepy things
Let crawl up to our feet the heats that will
Turn fire to burn.

  La R.   Your wisdom is too loud :
Doth it fear truly some court-card, some trick
That throws out honor ?

  Co.   Yea ; for note me this,
These men so wholly hate us and so well
It would be honey to their lips, I think,

To have our death for the familiar word
They chatter between mass-time and the bed
Wet with wine, scented with a harlot's hair,
They lie so smooth in.   When one hates like that,
So many of them, each a hand and mouth
To stab and lie and pray and poison with,
The bloodsmell quickens in the head, the scent
Feels gross upon the trail, and the steam turns
Thicker i' the noses of the crew; right soon
Shall their feet smoke in the red pasturing-place
And tongues lap hot; such cannot eat mere grass
Nor will drink water.

La R.   Are we stalled for them?
Are we their sheep? have we no steel? dumb sheep?

Co. No steel; the most of us have watered blood,
Their nerves are threads of silk, their talk such cries
As babies babble through the suckling milk,
Put them by these.

La R.   I have a way to help;
A damsel of the queen-mother's loves me
More than her mistress; she has eyes to kiss
That can see well; I 'll get us help of her.

Co. Tell her no word.

La R.   Yea, many words, I think.

Co. No word, sir, none.

La R.   This riddle sticks, my lord.

Co. To say we stand in fear is perilous prate;
To kneel for help would maim us in the feet,

So could we neither stand in time nor fly,
Being caught both ways. Do not you speak with her.

La R. I 'll make help somehow yet ; Yolande is good
And would not hurt us ; a fair mouth too small
To let lies in and learn broad tricks of speech ;
I 'll get help, surely. Does not your wound hurt ?

Co. Not much ; I pray you draw my cloak across ;
So ; the air chafes.

La R.   Go in and rest some while ;
Your blood is hot even to the fingers.

Co.   True ;
I shall sleep ill. Come in with me, fair lord.

> [*Exeunt.*

—◆—

ACT II.

SCENE I. *The Louvre.*

Enter King *and* DENISE.

Denise.

NAY, I shall know it.

Ch.   Tush ! you trouble me.

Den. O ay, I trouble you, my love 's a thorn
To prick the patience of your flesh away
And maim your silenced periods of whole sleep.
I will unlearn that love ; yea, presently.

Ch. What need I tell you ?

Den.   Trouble not your lip ;

I have no ear to carry the large news
That you shut up inside. Nay, go ; nay, go ;
It is mere pain, not love, that makes me dull ;
Count not on love ; be not assured of me ;
Trust not a corner of the dangerous air
With some lean alms of speech ; I may deceive you,
I may wear wicked color in the soul
When the cheek keeps up red. Perchance I lie.
    Ch. Thou art the prettiest wonder of God's craft ;
I think thy mother made thee out of milk,
Thy talk is such a maiden yet. Stay there, —
Are hands too costly for my fingering ? ha ?
    Den. Now I could kill you here between the eyes,
Plant the steel's bare chill where I set my mouth,
Or prick you somewhere under the left side ;
Why, thou man's face of cunning, thou live doubt,
Thou mere suspicion walking with man's feet !
Yea, I could search thy veins about with steel
Till in no corner of thy crannied blood
Were left to run red witness of a man,
No breath to test thee kinglier than dead flesh,
Sooner than lose this face to touch, this hair
To twist new curls in ; yea, prove me verily,
Sift passion pure to the blind edge of pain,
And see if I will — yet what need, what need ?
Kiss me ! there now, am I no queen for you ?
Here, take my fingers to mould flat in yours
That would mould iron flat, — eh, would not they ?

Ch. Ay, true, Denise, by God they can turn steel,
That 's truth now, — turn it like a bit of paste
Paddled each way, — that 's just short truth.
  Den.   Well, now,
That I do pray you put some trust on me
For love's fair merit and faith's noble sake,
What holds your lips so fast ? I should look proud,
Grave in the' mouth, with wise accomplice eyes,
A piece of your great craft. Make place for me ;
I pray you, place.
  Ch.   This counsel is more grave
Than death's lean face ; best your ear touch it not.
  Den. Nay then I will not ; for I would not pluck
So rough a knowledge on. · I am a child,
A show, a bauble kissed and laughed across ;
You lay your face over my head and laugh,
Your slow laugh underbreath runs in my hair.
Talk me of love, now ; there I understand,
Catch comprehension at the skirt of love,
Steal alms of it. Yet I would put love off
And rather make the time hard cover to me
Than miss trust utterly. But let that lie ;
Therein walks danger with both eyes awake,
Therefore no more. Tell me not anything.
  Ch. Thou shalt have all.
  Den.   Must I put violence
To war upon my words ? Have they said wrong ?
I was resolved not to distemper you.

Ch. Nay, I shall try your trust. Sit by me, so ;
Lay your hands thus. By God how fair you are,
It does amaze me ; surely God felt glad
The day he finished making you. Eh, sweet,
You have the eyes men choose to paint, you know ;
And just that soft turn in the little throat
And bluish color in the lower lid
They make saints with.

Den.   True. A grave thing to hear.

Ch. See yet, this matter you do fret me with
Seems no whit necessary, nor hath such weight,
Nor half the cost and value of a hair,
Poised with some perfect little wrath of yours
In fret of brows or lifting of the lip.
Indeed you are too precious for man's use,
Being past so far his extreme point of price,
His flawed and curious estimation,
As throws out all repute of words.

Den.   I would
My face were writhen like a witch ! Make forth.

Ch. Why, many a business feeds on blood i' the world,
And there goes many a knave to make a saint —

Den. I shall be angry. Sir, I am no fool,
But you do treat me as a dog might fare
Coming too near the fire.

Ch.   Nay, keep dry lids ;
I would not lose you for three days, to have
My place assured next God's. But see you now,

This gracious town with its smooth ways and walls
And men all mine in all of theirs —
 Den.   I see.
 Ch. This France I have in fee as sure as God
Hath me and you, — if this should fall to loss,
Were it no pity?
 Den.   Yea, sir, it were much.
 Ch. Or now, this gold that makes me up a king,
This apprehensive note and mark of time,
This token'd kingdom, this well-tested worth,
Wherein my brows exult and are begirt
With the brave sum and sense of kingliness,
To have this melted from a narrow head
Or broken on the bare disfeatured brows,
And marred i' the very figure and fair place
Where it looked nobly, — were this no shame to us?
 Den. Yea, this were piteous likewise.
 Ch.   Think on it.
For I would have you pitiful as tears,
Would have you fill with pity as the moon
With perfect round of seasonable gold
Fills her starved sides at point of the yellow month;
For if you leave some foolish part, some break,
Some idle piece or angle of yourself,
Not filled with wise and fearful pity up,
Then shame to hear the means of mine effect
Shall change you stone for good.
 Den.   I apprehend.

Ch. For I, by God, when I turn thought on it,
Do feel a heavy trembling in my sense,
An alteration and a full disease
As perilous things did jar in me and make
Contention in my blood.
　　Den. 　　　　　　Nay, but speak more;
Speak forth.　Good love, if I should flatter you —
　Ch. You see how hard and to what sharp revolt
The labor of the barren times is grown
Not in France merely, but in either land
That feels the sea's salt insolence on it;
The womb is split and shaken everywhere
That earth gets life of; and the taint therein
Doth like a venomous drug incite and sting
The sore unhealed rebellion in its house
To extreme working.　Now to supplant this evil
Doth ask more evil; men kiss not snakes to death,
Nor have we heard of bodies plagued to ache
Made whole with eating honey.　It is most good
That we should see how God doth physic time
Even to the quick and the afflictive blood
With stripes as keen as iron in the flesh.
Therefore, — That is, you have to apprehend
I mean no evil, but a righteous help;
I hate blood, too; indeed I love it not
More than a girl does.　Therefore it is hard.
Take note of me, I tell you it is hard.
　Den. I see.　Make on.

Ch.   It was to bring all right, —
And these men break God's smooth endurance up,
And he must hate them; and I love him so,
I and all friends, my mother here and all,
It hurts us, doth us wrong, puts pain on us,
When God forbears his cause to quit himself,
And gives no sign aside.

Den.   I may well think
These are your Huguenots that you do loathe;
You will do right upon them, will you not?

Ch. Ay, right, I will do right, nothing but right.
You are my absolute mistress and my choice,
The top and pearl of all mine ornament,
The golden and refined election
Of all the treasures I set hands to; well,
I do believe were you so mixed herein
As many are, many that I keep dear,
Dear and right precious in my just account,
And I had such a promise in God's ear
. As I have now to see an end of these,
I might renounce you too and give him leave
To make you parcel of the execution
That shall be done on these.

Den.   I fear you much;
For I can smell the mother in your speech,
This argument hath color of her eyes;
Where learnt you it?

Ch.   My brains do beat upon

3   D

The month's full time. Which day it is I know not;
It should look red upon the calendar,
And outblush its fierce use. The twenty-fourth of
    August, —
We stumble near it unawares by this ;
Give me the book.   *

Den.   What are you strayed upon ?
Ch. It is the time, the time, — you come too late
To tear its thread across.
Den.   Pray you, what time ?
Ch. But this Bartholomew shall be inscribed
Beyond the first; the latter speech of time
Shall quench and make oblivious war upon
The former and defeated memories,
New histories teaching it. For there will be
Blood on the moist untimely lip of death,
And in the dusty hunger of his bones
A sudden marrow shall refresh itself
And spread to perfect sinew. There will stir
Even in the red and hollow heat of hell
A motion of sharp spirit, a quickened sense
Such as wine makes in us ; yea, such a day
God hath not seen as I shall make for him.
Den. You put fear in me ; I can feel my blood
Go white with hearing you.
Ch.   We trap them all
In a great gin where the soul sticks as well.
Nay, there 's no hair of any Huguenot

But makes up parcel of my work in blood,
Nor face that is not painted with our swords.
(I told you this should hurt.) O, I could be
Most glad that I am taken to do this
And show the eyes of this lean world and time
The mould and the strong model of a king,
Not in the halting likeness of an ape
That fingers precious ware and knows it not,
From the teeth outward fool. Look you, I 'll do 't ;
Nay, as God stands beyond us twain, I will.
First Paris, — note you, Paris helps in it,
I stand not singly nerved, but in mine arm
Have multiplied the sinew of all these ;
France helps in it : the Guise has word to go
And take our admiral's patience by the throat
And finish the half issue of his blood ;
See, this side goes Tavannes ; here ride our men,
And here ; no falcon starved to bones and beak
Is tempered keener than our citizen
   Den. You will not murder them ?
   Ch.   Ay, will I not ?
I pray you tell me, was this well devised ?
   Den. You are changed foul with it : nay, stand more off;
Was it your meaning ?
   Ch.   Ay, mine, very mine ;
I will not lose it.
   Den.   Doth my sense hold fast ?
It is not possib'e you should do this

And scape the smell of blood. Nay, I but dream;
For if I wake, the substance of my flesh,
This form and fast impression of the air,
Yea, the most holy sun, are counterfeit;
We stick yards deeper than the foot of hell.
You see not well how foul a face you have, —
I will cry out on you.
    Ch.   Are you fallen mad?
    Den. I will put proclamation in the wind
That where but any shape of breath shall blow
It shall sound harsh as murder. Do you think
God shall sit fast and blink at you?
    Ch.   What more?
Get on; I do not chide you; nay, get breath;
Spare me no whit.
    Den.   I hate you beyond death;
Somewhat I had to say; give ear to me.
— It is all lost now, spilt in water, runs
Into sick tears. Forgive me my loud words,
I have much erred against your gracious game,
Mistaking all of you; I do confess
This jest so said has proved me dull and thick;
Now say it was well played and let me go.
You have played well indeed, and such hard parts —
Now I shall slip into mad speech again
And fail myself.
    Ch.   What is it you will do?
    Den. Alack, I see not that. Indeed I think

* It is God's will to kill me first i' the brain
And after in the flesh.   I am half mad.
But I can speak ; yea surely, I can speak ;
And I will cry in all the streets and make
Twinned correspondence 'twixt the tongued Seine banks
With sound and breath, clamor and noise of tears,
And windy witness of your enterprise.
O, you are moved now ; keep on that better face
And I will find some weeping way to you,
Persuading sin to peace ; you shall not do it ;
Lest all the recollection of men's lips
And noise of all just times and every place
That hath but any shape of good on it
Be sharp on you forever.

Enter the Queen-Mother *and* GUISE.

Ca.   So, you are loud,
I come betimes.   Sir, if you spare me room,
I have two words to say.
Ch.   I am bound to you ;
You have care of me indeed.   Bid her go in.
Ca. I would not be untimely.
Ch.   No, you are not,
You are a gracious mother, a good help.
(*To Denise.*) I 'll see you soon at night.
Den.   My lord, my lord —
Ca. Give my son breath at least ; you are impatient ;
It suits you not.

Gui. (*To the King.*) I wait upon your highness.

Ch. We are bounden to you too. Madam, go in.

[*Exit* DENISE.

Ca. My son, you put too large a face on this.

Ch. Mother, I put no face on it at all.
Come, pray you now, what do you look to get
By such a use of me ?

Ca.   You take strange ways
To chide me with ; I did expect your good.
Always it is the plague of love to be
Thus mated by some check. I will go play ;
Farewell.

Ch.   Nay, now you shall not go. My lord,
Tell her I meant no shame, no red i' the cheek ;
Say now I did not.

Ca.   I am content enough.
You may well see why we are come to you.

Ch. Yea, that I see.

Gui.   The men are at full point ;
Also the marshal helps us at all need
And some things over.

Ca.   You turn jealous of him.

Gui. Madam, I wear no envy on my words.

Ca. Sir, you are safe. Truly I am so glad
Now this thing clears i' the working and comes straight,
I could well jest and laugh.

Ch.   So could I not ;
All 's not squared yet ; you are too hot on it.

Ca. Too hot am I ?   Sir, you much wrong your honor
Taxing such heat in me ; I have proof of you,
So hath the Guise, that you have wrought herein
As hard as any.
Gui.   I take your part as mine
For witness of my lord's free grace and will
Towards this matter.
. *Ch.*   *This matter,* — call it so ;
Have you such honey in the mouth, my lord,
To make a milky matter of the name ?
Why, if men are to call us murderers,
Let 's take the word up and not tell such lies,
Skulking with beaten cheeks behind the word.
Gui. (Aside to Cath.) He is touched the wrong side yet.
Ca. (Aside to Guise.) I have stung myself ;
This girl I set on him has thrown us out,
Played her own way. That we should pay such apes
To pinch us in the wrist !
Ch.   What are you saying?   '
Ca. Take your best means : here 's none shall cross
    you, sir.
We do but say if you will give them leave
To slit your throat with whispering, — or abed
Take medicine of them, — or wear gloves of theirs, —
Or please your mouth with drinking after them, —
It is no matter.
Ch.   Would you have me mad ?
I have not heard of such a tax on them ; *

No, not since Florence taught us to use drugs
Has it been noised of these.

 Ca.   I think indeed
That poison hath no Florence in the drug
Which puts the peril of so hard a speech
In my son's lip. Do not unsay it ; no :
I do not bid you take the blur from me.
I am content to stay and take shame up
So I may suit you. O sweet son, — my lord,
Forgive me that my tongue so slips on you,
Catching the old name first, — I pray you note
That I can be as patient as your ear
Hath been of me too long. This is the last
That I shall ever take of words to push
Your just forbearance beyond use. I said
" Farewell " as idly as one says " good thanks "
To him that hath not earned it : but I see
Here is made room for a farewell indeed.
Now could I take it silently and go,
Turning my very passion to content
And no whit using it : I am not abashed,
Albeit I speak as one whom shame has marred ;
That I am not I pray take no offence,
For should I show a penitent herein
I must do penance for much care of you,
And this I will not. Be not offended with me ;
For God doth know, sweet son, that in my life
I have used many days in loving you.

Consider of it : I do not boast myself,
Seeing I but fall within the range and scope,
The limit and fair marge of a good law ;
Yet if I have not been there excessive (as
I say not that I have one whit exceeded),
Surely I have not shortened its just room
Or narrowed in the sweet law's offices.
That I am so put off I say is well ;
You are wise herein ; for women at best count
Are the mere spoil of a male reason, lie
In his loosest thoughts outside. We are the chaff,
The gross unwinnowed husks of your fanned wheat ;
I say that you do well to turn me off.
But this too for my witness I should say ;
That if you do me there a word of wrong,
Yea the thin grain of one particular word,
The same is worse than ill. I pardon it.
That I did love you, God shall do me right
To bring the credit will approve it me :
That I have sought your health yourself believe ;
That I did love the state and would get ease
For its wried body, shall make smooth my name
In patient reputation of good men.
The end of that is come. Sir, this much yet;
Since you have thus delivered up your place,
Your worth and body to the love of these
That hate me deadly — wherein you do well,
For yet I will not say but you do well —

3*

‚

I will entreat such almsgiving of you
As for my son of Anjou and myself
May serve to make us a safe place away,
Where we may keep behind the perilous time
And house with simple peace. For I do know
That howsoe'er these fare as friends with you,
With us they will but fare as murderers do
That live between the sharpening of a knife
And the knife's edge imbrued. This being made sure,
I take my leave of a most royal care
That has been precious pain to me, and is
No costlier than a pin. The end is here
That I have gladly answered.
    Ch.   You say well;
I would not have you think so thinly of me
As that girl's mercy and the feeble flesh
Prevail upon advice. I love you much.
But me she heeds not; tell her you, my lord,
I love no meddled policy of man's
Before her honor.
    Ca.   I am perfect in your way.
Best let me part more quickly.
    Ch.   You shall not go.
    Gui. Madam, your son is tempered graciously ;
You see his will keeps good.
    Ch.   Ay, so it doth ;
I thank you, sir ; you see my will is good.
    Ca. I had rather be a thing of laboring days
Than a so childed mother.

Gui.   You must give her way.

Ca. It is not fit that I should wear your time.

Ch. That year of mine is lame wherein you lack.

Ca. Nay, there 's no speech of silk will serve your turn,
You must be whole with me or break; I 'll have
No patched alliance, lank allegiances,
Starved out of use.

Ch.   I do not like the business.

Ca. Nay, but speak large; what is it you mislike?

Ch. Keep you that way.

Ca.   Why this is what I said.

Ch. I have thought of it, and have informed my heart
How pale distempering evil makes the blood
That ran full way before. I will not do it;
Lest all that regiment of muffled years
Now huddled in the rear and skirts of time
I must walk through, take whips into their hands
To bruise my shame withal.

Ca.   I heed you not.
It is the sick and infirm spite of fear
Makes your will insolent. But as it please you;
It is not I that shall wear death for it.

Gui. You do both stray: give me some leave to speak,
And keep your patience whole. Right noble sir,
For my poor worth and special reverence here
I would not waste the price of half an hour;
Though I might say, and no man cross the lie,
That in the personal state of mine esteem

I have kept endurance on against a wrong
That might put blood i' the dead.   My royal father,
Whose cost did earn the sum of such a name,
Yea, even to full repute ; whose motive hand
Did the most inward ties of war unloose,
And pluck its joint away ; this man so built,
So strained and clean of any weak revolt
That faith herself did set her tongue by his
And use his lesson for her proper text ;
This bulk and nerve of all your services
Fashioned in one man's work ; how he came dead
You twain are no whit less assured than I,
Who have thrown beyond conjecture.   It is poor truth
To say we think that he fared treacherously ;
If knowledge be no weaker than report,
And proof no looser than a popular mouth,
Then we do know it.   O, such a want we have,
So dear and so entire a loss in him,
As should make France the book of all men's griefs,
The mould wherein a very face of sorrow
Were cast indeed.   That I have not avenged him,
Both you dare swear : that it is not my shame,
But my sore pain and burden of this time,
Both you do likewise see.   How say you, sir !
Will you find sufferance smoother-faced than mine ?
Have I borne much ? or is there fault in me,
Who am the limit of endurances ?
Now in this very point of patience here,

Even here, you take me ; and considering this,
Commend the calm and heaviness in me
That lackeys your own purpose, runs before
Your proper care, pages your policy.
Now, sir,
Were I a poor man's dog the same were well ;
Were I a sick man's fool the same were well ;
Being thus, I doubt it is not well at all.
A father slain is more than so much bones
That worms and flies dishallow, being thin dust
And out of value ; and personally to me
It is much more.   I will not have this way ;
Lest my most loving honor borne to you
Leave me ashamed, or service done disbark
All graces from me.   You were strongly sworn,
Yea, with the assurance that all faith makes up,
To help us mend the ravelled rents of time ;
But though you had more iron in your hand
Than you have yet, you cannot grasp therein
Two faiths, two sides, two justices at once.
Choose you, and put good will to choice ; for me,
I am not thralled in your election.

   Ch. Madam, his talk flies far.

   Ca.   True, he speaks right.

   Ch. Should I not answer with a lip more tame,
This friendship might turn slack.

   Gui.   I keep still loyal.

   Ch. Yea, sir, we doubt you nothing, nothing at all :

You are our lawful friend ; you speak all well ;
You have had wrong, men use you grievously ;
And I do love you for your bearing it.

    Ca. The man that slew Duke Francis has his breath.

    Ch. Ay, and his blood, some scantlings too of that :
We saw what tithe of it was spilled in him.
Still it is quaint that such a shaken scalp,
So gray as that, should cover so much red ;
'T is very strange and quaint ; ha, think you not ?

    Ca. (*To Guise.*) All's clear again ; he smells about the
        blood
That shall incense his madness to high strain ;
Look, now he peers and fingers on his sleeve.

    Gui. Pish ! it looks ugly.

    Ca.   I must push him yet,
Make his sense warm.   You see, blood is but blood ;
Shed from the most renowned veins o' the world,
It is no redder ; and the death that strikes
A blind broad way among the foolish heaps
That make a people up, takes no more pains
To finish the large work of highest men ;
Take heart and patience to you ; do but think
This thing shall be no heavier then, being done,
Than is our forward thought of it.

    Ch.   Ay true,
But if men prate of blood — I 'll none on me.
And yet I care not much.   You are wise, mother ;
You know me through, ay, and know God as well,
Whom I know not.   This is a grave thing.

Ca.   Yea,
And graver should be if I gave you way.
What are you made God's friend for but to have
His hand over your head to keep it well
And warm the rainy weather through, when snow
Spoils half the world's work ? shall I let you go
And slip your boy's neck from God's hold on it
To graze and get mere pasture like a beast ?
Nay, child, there 's nothing better for a man
Than to trust God ; why, must I tell you that ?
Is there more beard than blood in cheeks like this
Till some one smite them ?   Now I think, I think
And praise God for it, the next Huguenot
Who plucks you by the ear or smites on the face
Shall do no much work after.

Ch.   True, madam,
I need be king now ; you speak true in that.

Ca. I 'll call you king then always, king and son,
Dear son and lord of mine.   Hold fast on this
And you are man indeed, and man enough
To teach command to the world and make its back
Stoop for allegiance.   See you, my fair son,
This sweet face of authority is a mask
For slaves to rivet or undo the joint,
Except one wear it in the eyes of them
A witness to outbear shame and revolt
And maim resistance in the hands ; you were
Never yet king, never had will to wear

That circle that completes the head with gold
And shuts up strength inside the hold of it ;
You are now made man.

 Ch.   And you made mother twice,
Not by gross generation of the womb,
But issue of more princely consequence ;
Set this day gold upon your writ of life,
The last of child-bearing for you ; so God
Give you good time of it !

 Ca.   Ay, grace to thank
That grace that gives not mere deliverance
From unrespective burdens of the flesh,
But the keen spirit refines and recreates
To gracious labor.   That God that made high things,
He wrought by purpose and secure design
The length of his contrivance ; he set not tigers
In the mean seat of apes, nor the wild swine
I' the stabled post of horses ; birds and dogs
Find portion of him, and he sets the fish
In washing waters ; rain and the sweet sun
He shuts and opens with his hand ; and us
Hath he set upright and made larger eyes
To read some broken letters of this book
Which has the world at lesson ; and for what,
If we not do the royalest good work,
If we not wear the worth of sovereignty
As attribute and raiment ?   At our feet
Lies reason like a hound, and faith is chained ;
Lame expectation halts behind our ways,

The soundless secret of dead things is made
As naked shallows to us. It is for that
We owe strong service of the complete soul
To the most cunning fashioner that made
So good work of us ; and except we serve,
We are mere beasts and lesser than a snake,
Not worth his pain at all ; so might we shift
The soul as doth that worm his colored back,
And turn to herd with footless things that are
The spoil of dust and rain. To close up all,
Death takes the flesh in his abhorréd hands
Of clean alike and unclean ; but to die
Is sometimes gracious, as to slip the chain
From wrist and ankle ; only this is sad,
To be given up to change and the mere shame
Of its abominable and obscure work
With no good done, no clean thing in the soul
To sweeten against resurrection-time
This mire that made a body, lest we keep
No royalties at all, or in the flesh
The worm's toothed ravin touch the soul indeed.

   Ch. Madam, I hold your sentence good to hear ;
I 'll do as you would have me. Pray you now,
Make no more record of my foolishness.
I have used idle words. Make count of me
As of your servant ; for from this day forth
I 'll hold no Huguenot's throat one whit more worth
Than is the cord upon it. Sir, good day.   [*Exit* King.

E

Ca. I told you this before ; sit down and laugh.
I told you this should be.

Gui.   We have worked well.

Ca. Is this no better now than violent ways
To threaten the poor passage of his life
With the mean loss of some sick days and hours ?
You would not let him fill his season up
And feed on all his portions cut i' the world ;
You have iron in your policies, and hate
The unbound brows of composition ;
But I, whose cheek is patient of all wrongs,
Who have endurance to my garment, worn
In face o' the smiters, I know through by heart
Each turn i' the crannies of the boy's spoilt mind
And corner used in it. Years gone, my lord,
Before the tender husk of time grew hard,
He would make pastime to tear birds to death
And pinch out life by nips in some sick beast ;
And being a man, blood turns him white to see.
Believe me that, I 'll praise you more for faith
Than I praise God for making him a fool.
What shall get done though hell stand up to hear
And in God's heaven God's self become ashamed,
The rule of use rebel against its way,
The sense of things upon itself revolt,
To the undoing of man, — this shall not fail
For the meek sake of his most female mouth
That would keep honey in.

Gui.   Have your way so :
I do not cross you ; keep that fashion.
   Ca.   Yea,
I think to have it certainly, fair sir ;
Keen man he were that should cheat me of it.
  Gui. This screw of yours has wrenched him round our
      way ;
Yet these may pinch the wax, new-mould his face,
Carve him a mouth, make here an eye or there ;
Will you wring loose their fingers till he drop
Like a fruit caught, so, in one's hollowed hand ?
You 'll have some necks to break across ere that.
Why, Châtillon's gray chin keeps wagging down
Close at his ear ; that demi-dog Soubise
Is made his formal mirth ; fool Pardaillan
Struts with his throat up like a cock's, and brags
The king is kind, — has secrets, — he might say
Some grace was done him, — would not miss his luck. —
As for the merit —
   Ca.   So far it goes by rote ;
Were there no larger peril than hangs there,
I 'd strangle it with but a hair of mine.
  Gui. Madam, I would be fain to understand.
  Ca. Sir, this it is ; the woman I set on
To shape and stoop him perfectly my way,
Is very falsely made my thorn, and wears
Such fashions as a new-enfranchised slave
To beat his master for delivering him.

She is turned milk, would slit her web mis-made
Now it shows blood at edge.

Gui.   What ailed your judgment then
To light on her ? had you some plague i' the eye
To choose so sickly ?

Ca.   The king did lean to her,
And out of his good will I made this cord
To lead him by the ear.   Do not you doubt me ;
She has not slit the web so near across
But her own edge may turn upon her skin :
I have a plot to rid the time of her
For some slight days.

Gui.   Some trick to bite her life ?

Ca. Nay, I 'll not lose her ; no more weight shall be
Than a new time may lift from her again.
I shall but get a clog upon my court
Slyly removed ; a double good shall bud
Upon a most small evil.   Go with me
And bring me to my women.   [*Exeunt.*

SCENE II.   *The Admiral's House.*

Enter COLIGNY *and* Attendant.

Co. Carry these letters to my son, and bid him
Attend me with La Noue.   If you shall see
That noble man who spoke with me to-day,
Pray him be with me too.   This is a care

That I would have you diligent in ; so shall you
Gather fresh good of me.

Att.   I will, my lord.

Co. I shall be bound to you ; the time that makes
Such ruin of us doth yet bequeath me this,
That where I find good service without break,
I hold it dearer than a prosperous man.
See you be speedy.

Att.   I am already hence.   [*Exeunt.*

SCENE III.   *The Louvre.*

Enter LA ROCHEFOUCAULD *and* YOLANDE DE MONTLITARD.

La R. You do not use me smoothly.

Yol.   Did I sue
That you would love me ?   I owe you nothing.

La R.   •   No ?
But if I leave with you so much of me,
Do I not keep some petty part of you ?

Yol. O, not a whit ; what would you do with it ?

La R. In faith, I know not.

Yol.   You have the holy way
Of cutting clean an oath ; as you do coin it
A girl might use the like ; your protestation
Is made out of the ravel of spoilt silk ;
I trust no such tagged speech.

La R.   To do you pleasure
I would unswear the seated saints from heaven

And put shame out of use with violent breath.
But to my point.

Yol.   Shall I not say one thing?

La R. So I would have you.

Yol.   Then I think, this breath
So spent on my vexation is not used
For love of me — nay, pray, you keep that in —
But the keen service of your admiral
To whom I must be evidenced.

La R.   What then?
Are you too far in hate to do me good?

Yol. Too far in faith to swell you with such help;
Put down i' the writing that a woman's trust
Is much belied with you; there's no such flaw
As male repute doth work to blot us with;
I swear I will not show you anything.

La R. I do not beg such alms of you; come back:
Do words make all the sweet on so sweet lips?

Yol. I did not bid you shift your note to this.
Sir, that ring's edge of yours has cut my glove.   [*Exeunt.*

ACT III.

SCENE I. *Environs of the Louvre.*

Enter DENISE.

Denise.

BID me keep silence? though I lose all, I'll wear
  Silence no further on my wrong-doings
That holds no weather out. I'll speak then; God,
Keep me in heart to speak! because my sense,
Even to the holiest inward of its work
This unclean life has marred; I am stained with it
Like a stained cloth, it catches on my face,
Spoils my talk midways, breaks my breath between,
Paints me ill colors, plucks me upon the sleeve,
As who would say, "Forget me will you, then?"
Bid me keep silence? yea, but in losing that
Lies are so grown like dirt upon my lip
No kisses will wipe dry nor tears wash bare
The mouth so covered and made foul. Dear God,
I meant not so much wrong-doing that prayer
Should choke or stab me in the throat to say;
For see, the very place I pray withal
I use for lying and put in light words
To soil it over: the thoughts I make prayer with
Fasten on ill things and set work on them,
Letting love go. If one could see the king
And escape writing —

Enter CINO.

Cino.   Yea, cousin, at prayer so late ?
Teach me the trick, I would be fain to pray,
I grow so sick now with the smell of time.
Ah, the king hurts you? touch a spring i' the work
And it cries — eh? and a joint creaks in it ?

Den. This fool wears out.

Cino.   At wrists ?

Den.   At head ; but, fool,
Hast thou not heard of the king?

Cino.   Yea, news, brave news ;
But I 'll not spoil them on you.

Den.   My good Cino —
Nay, sweet thing, fair sir, any precious word,
Tell me.

Cino. The king — what will you give me then?
Half a gold fringe worn off your cloak for alms ?

Den. Nay, anything it wills, my Cino. Quick.

Cino. A ring? yea, more ; what's better than a ring ?
A kiss I doubt of yours ; but I 'll have best,   .
Nothing of good or better.

Den.   Come, sir ; well ?

Cino. Tell me what's better than a kiss ; but hear you ;
Pull not away, paint me no red ; the king —

Den. What is the king?

Cino.   Twice half his years, I think ;
God keep him safe between the grays and blacks.

Den. My head is full of tears and fever ; hence,

Get from me, fool. Thou ragged skirt of man,
Thou compromise 'twixt nothing and a bat!
Blind half a beast! I 'd see thee hanged and laugh.
What fool am I to scold at thy brain's shell?
What sort of under thing shall I call thee,
Who am thy railer?

Cino.   What would you have me? ha?
Must I poison my poor bread or choke myself
To make French Chicot room?   Being simply fool,
I eat fool's alms: I may talk wise men down,
Who gives me sober bread to live by? see;
You 'll let me prate now?

Den.   Yea, prate anything;
Find me the queen, and I 'll with you.   Cino —

Cino. Well?

Den.   Use me better as we go, poor fool.

                                        [*Exeunt.*

Enter King, TAVANNES, PARDAILLAN, SOUBISE, BRANTÔME,
                    and others.

Ch. Brown hair or gold, my lord Soubise, you say?

Sou. Pure black wears best.

Par.   He will not say so, sir.

Ch. Ay, will not? are you wise, my Pardaillan?

Bra. Yolande — you know this damozel I mean,
One that has black hair hard on blue —

Sou.   Hear that!
Blue hair, eyes black!

Bra.   But note me what she says:

4

Soubise is a fair name, and that fair lord
That wears it sewn across his arm is good
To give her tame bird seeds to eat.
    Sou.   Her bird!
    Bra. She has a sister of your height, this girl,
Skilled to work patterns with gold thread and paint.
    Sou. Well, what of her then?
    Ch.   Yea, sir, hold by that.
    Bra. She said this to me, choosing seeds of corn
To put between her peacock's bill, it chanced,
One summer time; and biting with her teeth
Some husk away to make the grain more soft,
She put her mouth to the bird's mouth : but I —
"Give me food rather, I have need to eat";
Whereat her teeth showed fuller and she said
— The seed still in her lip — she laughed and said
Her two tame birds, this peacock and Soubise,
Were all she had to feed.
    Sou.   I thank her.
    Ch.   Well,
What followed? that you kissed away the seed?
    Bra. Hush now, she comes, fair lord.

♪Enter Queen-Mother, DENISE, YOLANDE, *and other Ladies,*
with CINO.

    Ca.   Take heart, Denise;
I'll chide him home. — Fair son, I hear hard news;
My lord of Guise in his ill hours of blood

Will hardly trust your courtesy to use
His lady's glove : here was one wept right out
At hearing of it.
    Ch.   He does belie my patience ;
It was this lord that had her glove away.
    Ca. The Guise is sick of it, touched hard and home ;
It bites him like a hurt ; you are his keen plague,   .
Sharp sauce to hunger, medicine to his meat,
A sufferance no pained flesh could hold upon
And not turn bitter.
    Ch.   Well, God heal his head !
    Ca. I did not see my lord Soubise — make room,
So thick a yellow crowd of ladies' heads
Makes the air taste of powdered scent and spice
One cannot see a friend ; my lord Soubise,
We love you well, what holds you back, my lord ?
    Sou. Madam —
    Ca.   They trouble us with tales of you ;
Here's a maid carries face of Montlitard
Whose heart seems altered to a fresher name
The blood paints broader on her cheek, sweet fool ;
Answer me this ; nay, I shall make you clear ;
Denise has told me how her middle sleep
Was torn and broken by lamentings up,
By sudden speeches, shreds and rags of talk,
And running over of light tears between ;
And ever the poor tender word " Soubise "
Sighed and turned over — ah, such pain she had !
Poor love of mine, why need you spoil me her ?

Sou. She will not say so.

Yol. But she will not say
She loves not, though it sting her soul to speak,
Being still, woe 's me, so sharp and sore a truth
And hard to hide.

Ch. Well said of her ; strike hands.

Cino. Take comfort, daughter ; he shall be made fast
    to thee
And the Devil climbs not in by way of marriage.
Conclude temptation, and God increase your joy
In the second generation of good fools.
Gripe fingers each ; I will be bridesman ; so.

Sou. Fool — I am hurt with wonder, madam — fool —

Cino. Nay, sir, keep hands.

Ch. This is most gross in you.

Cino. Yea, so ; this is the time of horn-blowing.
Did your grace never eat stolen eggs ? the meat of them
Is something like the mouth of a fair woman.
Beseech you now let your priest drink no wine
And you shall have him better for yourself ;
Sir, look to that ; I would not have you marred.

Ch. No, you shall stay.

Sou. I pray you, bid him peace.

Ch. Let the fool talk.

Cino. There 's freedom for your kind now.
I have not seen a groom so blench and start ;
I wonder what shoe pinched his mother ?

Sou. Beast ! [*Strikes him, and exit.*

Ca. You are sad, sir.

Ch. I am not well at heart.

Ca. It is the summer heat ; I have not seen
So hard a sun upon the grape-season
These twelve years back. — Fellow, look up, take heart ;
He cannot hurt thee.

Cino. Why not ? I am no woman.
I am sure he has made my head swell ; get him married,
I 'll do as much for him. Eh ? will I not ? (*To Yolande.*)

Yol. I will not wed him ; so the shame shall stick
Where it began, on him alone.

Ca. (*Aside.*) Whispers ?

(*Observing Denise and the King.*)

I do suspect you sorely. Oh ! so close ;
Thrusting your lip even against his ear ?
Yea, hold the sleeve now, pinch it up; (*aloud*) there may be
No ill in this ; and I have hope it wears
No face of purpose, but I like it not.

Yol. What is it you mislike ?

Ca. Eh ? nothing, I ;
My care 's not half the worth of a fool's head
Nor carries so much weight. My lord Bourdeilles,
Have you no tale for us ?

Bra. Yea, madam, a rare jest.

Yol. We 'll pluck it forth.

Renée. Ay, pinch it out of him ;
We would be merry.

Par. Umph ! I know the tale.

Bra. I would not have a gospeller hear you, sir.

Cino. I see a tale now hang at the king's sleeve.

Ca. A very light one.

Bra.   But if you hear me, madam, —

There 's matter for a leap-year's laugh therein.

The noble damsel of Maulévrier —

Ca. Is she your tale ?

Bra.   Speak low ; she told it me.

Yol. Where should he hear it ?

Ca.   Peace now : sir, make on.

Bra. She being about my lady of Navarre

Last night, — I mean some foolish nights ago,

For there last night she was not, I believe, —

Made out this jest : this is the jest she made.

Cino. 'T is a sweet jest, but something over ripe.

Bra. You have not heard it.

Cino. I hear it with my nose, and it smells rank.

Bra. You all do know his highness of Navarre

Is loving to his lady ; and, God's death,

She is worth no less a price ; nor doth affection,

Being set on her, outweigh the measured reason

Nor sense of limit she doth well deserve ;

Yea, she outgoes the elected best, outswells

What is called good.

Cino.   A very merry tale.

Bra. Prithee, fool, peace. — Now at that time I speak of

He was at point to come ; but being delayed

(The how I say not — this I do not say ;

Indeed I would not — mark you, not the how)
He could not come. She, grown hereon to heat,
Chid at her ladies, wrangled with her hair,
Drew it all wried, then wept, then laughed again ;
Till one saying, " Madam, I did see my lord
About the middle matter of the dusk
Slip forth to speak with " — here she stayed ; the queen
Doth passionately catch her by that word,
Crying with whom ? and might this be a man ?
And should men use her so ? and shame of men,
And not the grace of temperance in them
Which is the cover and the weeds of sin ;
And such wet circumstance of waterish words
As ladies use ; whereto the damsel — " Madam,
I may swear truly no man had him forth,
But to swear otherwise — "
    Ca.   I do perceive you;
There was a conference of the gospellers,
And there was he.
    Bra.   But he that brought him forth —
    Ca. Enough, the jest runs out ; I know your matter.
Fair son, you would be private ?
    Ch.   Like enough :
I do not say you trouble me to stay,
But you shall please me going.
    Ca.   Good time to you !
Come with me, sirs. Take you the fool along.
              [*Exeunt all but* King *and* DENISE.

Ch. I am assured you love me not a whit.

Den. You will not set your faith upon that thought ;
I love you dearly.

Ch.   I do not bid you swear it.

Den. I pray you, if you know what I would say,
That you endure this feebleness which sits
Upon my lips i' the saying.

Ch.   What do you think of me ?

Den. I know you are my master, and a king
That I have called thrice nobler than his name ;
I know my lip hath got the print of you,
And that the girdle of your fastened arms
Keeps warm upon me yet ; and I have thought,
Yea, I have sworn it past the reach of faith,
Even till the temperate heaven did, stung at me,
Begin a chiding, — that you loved me back
To the large aim and perfect scope o' the heart ;
That I was as a thing within your blood,
There moved, and made such passage up and down
As doth the breath and motion of your air ;
Being rather as a pain caught unawares,
A doubtful fever or sick heat of yours
That now the purging time hath rid you of
And made smooth ease.

Ch.   You did know better then.

Den. Nay, then I think I knew not anything;
My wits were broken in the use of love.
What do you think of me ?   I would know that.

Ch. As of a thing I love — I know not what;
Only that any slight small thing of yours,
A foolish word, a knot upon your head,
Some plait worn wrong or garment braced awry,
Any girl's thing — doth grow so and possess
With such a strength of thought, so waxen full,
The complete sum and secret of my will
I cannot get it out.

Den.   If that be love,
Then I love you, which you did swear a lie.
For I do feed upon you in my meat
And sleep upon you in my tired bed
And wake upon you in my praying times,
As you were used and natural unto me,   •
My soul's strong habit and nativity.

Ch. I think you do : I never taxed you else.
But he that will not swear I love you back
Doth sin outside the heavy name of lie
And compass of a villain.

Den.   I doubt you not.
You know that I did urge you for the queen?

Ch. Yea : you made up a peace between our jars.

Den. Ay, like a damnéd peacemaker, a truce
More sharp than is the naked side of war.

Ch. What now? you slip on that fool's text again?

Den. That I did pluck you over to her side
I would repent even in the cost and price
Of my most inward blood, yea of my heart.

4*   F

Ch. You did a good work then : now you turn sharp.

Den. I do well think that had I never been
You had not fallen in her purposes.

Ch. I may perceive my patience is your fool :
You make slight use of me.   Take note of this,
Henceforth I will not undergo the words
That it shall please you cast upon my place
In such loose way.   What makes you chide at me ?
Have you no sort of fool but me to wear
The impatient work of your mistempered blood
With a soft spirit ?

Den.   You have sworn me love ;
If you did love me with more worth and weight
Than slackly binds a two hours' liking up,
You would not pluck displeasure from my words.
I am too weak to make fit wrath for you.

Ch. Ay, that I think.

Den.   You do me right ; but mark,
Being this I am, not big enough to hurt,
I do repent me past all penitence,
Outweep the bounded sorrow of all words,
That I did bring you to such peace again
As hath its feet in blood.

Ch.   You did then swear
Nothing one half so blessed and so clean
As to make peace between her lips and mine ;
You bade me think how good it was to have
The grace of such a gentle fellowship

To lean my love upon ; how past the law
And natural sweetness of sweet motherhood
Her passion did delight itself on me ;
With all the cost of rare observances
Followed the foot of my least enterprise ;
Esteemed me even to the disvaluing
Of her own worthy life ; would not, in brief,
Partake the pain of common offices
And due regard that custom hath of time
But for my love. Was this no talk of yours ?
 Den. Indeed I said so.
 Ch.   Did I not give you faith ?
 Den. You did believe me ; I would you had not so,
Or that some poisonous pain had killed my lips
Before they learnt the temper of such words.
 Ch. What then, you knew not this red work indeed ?
No savor of this killing flecked your speech ?
 Den. I know of it ? but to have lied and known
I had been plagued past all the gins of hell.
I know of it ? but if I knew of it
There is no whip that God could hunt me with
That would not seem less heavy than thin snow
Weighed with the scars and shames of my desert.
 Ch. But how if such a thing be necessary ?
 Den. There 's no such need that bids men damn them-
  selves.
 Ch. Nay, but if God take hell to work withal
That is more bitter than all waste of men,

And yet God makes the honey of his law
Out of its sharp and fire-mouthed bitterness,
Why may not I take this ? yea, why not I ?

Den. If you shall think on murder, how it is,
How mere a poison in all mouths of men
That only at the casual use of it
Sicken and lose the rule of their discourse,
Being wounded with it ; how poorest men alive
That in dull drink have chanced upon a life
Are slain for it, and the red word of sin
Doth elbow them at side and dig their grave
And makes all tongues bitter on them, all eyes
Fills out with chiding — how very knaves do loathe
The tax and blot of such a damnéd breath
As goes to call hard murder by his name ;
Yea, how blood slain shall not be healed again,
Never get place within the ruined veins,
Never make heat in the forsaken flesh ;
O, you shall think thereon.

Ch.   Have I not thought ?

Den. Not this I bid you, this you have not thought ;
How to each foot and atom of that flesh
That makes the body of the worst man up
There went the very pain and the same love
That out of love and pain compounded you,
A piece of such man's earth ; that all of these
Feel, breathe, and taste, move and salute and sleep,
No less than you, and in each little use

Divide the customs that yourself endure ;
And are so costly that the worst of these
Was worth God's time to finish ; O, thus you shall not,
Even for the worth of your own well-doing,
Set iron murder to feed full on them.

   Ch. Fret me no more ; I shall turn sharp with you.

   Den. O, sir, in such dear matter as I have
I fear not you at all. You shall not go.

   Ch. I may forget your body's tender make
And hurt you. Do not put me from myself ;
I am dangerous then; being sobered, I do know
How rash and sharp a blood I have, and weep
For my fierce use of it: push not so far.

   Den. Yea now, put all the bruise of them on me
And I will thank you. You did hurt me once,
Look here, my wrist shows where you plucked it hard ;
I never spoke you ill for it ; you shall
Do me worse hurt and I not cry at all.

   Ch. This is fool's talk.

   Den.   And once in kissing me
You bit me here above the shoulder, yet
The mark looks red from it ; you were too rough,
I swore to punish you and starve your lip
To a more smooth respect. I have loved you, sir ;
Sir, this is harsh that you regard me not.

   Ch. Nay, peace ! I will not have you loud.

   Den.   My lord —

   Ch. Say " Charles " now ; be more tender of your mouth.

Den. Sir, the shame that burns through my cheek and
  throat
Cannot get words as hot as blood to speak,
Or you would hear such ; keep your eyes on me,
Ay, look so ; have you sense or heart, my lord ?
Are you not sorry if one come to wrong ?
  Ch. This is some trap. What makes you turn so quick :
  Den. Yea, king, are you ? yea, is this not the king ?
And I so pray, speak words so hard to speak,
Kneel down, weep hard, — but you shall hear this out, —
To be put like a garment off? not so.
The queen-mother throws nets about, spins well,
Contrives some thread to strike the whole web through,
To catch you like a plague, — there 's worse and worse, —
What hurt is it, what pain to men outside,
Although she ruin us, make spoil of us,
Melt the gold crown into a ring of hers,
What harm ?
  Ch.   What harm by God! I think much harm.
  Den. But this is worse — to catch France in her trap,
People and all, body and soul ; cheat God,
Ruin us all, as ruined we shall be,
I know not how too well, but something thus,
And now God puts this hour of time to be
A steel sword in your hand, and says withal,
" Now give me token if there be a king
Inside you, do me right who made you way,
Drew you so high " ; I pray you for God's love

Let none put thievish fingers on the time,
Loosen your sword God girt so next your side.
What, men steal money and you hang for that,
What, one puts just his little knife in you
As I put just a bodkin in this hair,
And he gets choked with cord and spat upon —
But when some treason stabs belief in the back,
Thrusts its tongue out and wags its head at God,
Turns bitter his sweet mouth with vinegar,
Bruises him worse than any Pilate's Jews,
These men go free ? It were too hard to think.
Yea, sir, I will not have you lift your lip,
Yea, you may smite me with your foot, fair lord,
Whom yesterday you kissed here in the mouth ;
I lay no care on life or on this breath
Or on this love that hath so dead an end ;
More ill is done than good will ever be,
And I now pluck the finished fruit of it
Planted by bitter touches of the lip,
False breath, hot vows, the broken speech of lust,
By finger-pinches and keen mouths that bite
Their hard kiss through: nay, but I pray you well
Let there be no more ill than grows hereon,
No such kiss now that stings and makes a stain,
No cups drunk out that leave dead lees of blood.
Be sorry for me ; yea, be good, my king,
Tender with me: let not the queen-mother
Touch me to hurt: sir, know you certainly

None loves you better : also men would say
It may be some joy you have had of me ;
Even for that sake, for that most evil sake,
Have some good mercy.

    Ch.   Mad, but really mad !
Here, child, put up your hands in mine, Denise :
By God's blood, the girl shakes and shakes and burns —
What, have you fever ?

    Den.   None, no pain ; but, sir,
Be pitiful a little ; my sweet lord,
Have you not had me wholly in one hand
To do your will with ? would I lie to you ?

    Ch. Eh, would you lie ? well, God knows best, I doubt.

    Den. I pray God bring me quick to bitter hell
If I lie to you : have you eyes at least ?
That woman with thin reddish blood-like lips,
That queen-mother that would use blood for paint,
Can you not see her joint the trap for you,
Not see the knife between her fingers, sir,
Where the glove opens ?

    Ch.   This is right your way ;
A sweet way, this ; what will you bid me do ?

    Den. Not this, not this she pulls you on to do ;
Not set a treason where a promise was,
Not fill the innocent time with murder up,
Not —

    Ch. Tush ! some preacher's plague has caught the child.
Are you mad truly ? some strange drink in you ?

Den. Sir —

Ch.   Do you take me for no king at all,
That you talk this ?   I never heard such talk.
No hands on me ; nay, go, and have good day.

                                      [*Exit* DENISE.

Re-enter the Queen-Mother *and* YOLANDE.

Do you note this, our mother ?
Ca.   Yea, and well.
Ch. This is the very mercy of a maid ;
To cut a hand off lest a finger ache
And paint the face of resolution white
Lest the red startle one.
Ca.   It is most true ;
I pray you be not movable of wit
Or waxen to her handling.
Ch.   I will not ;
There 's nothing shall have time to startle me,
Being in this work so deep ; no delicate sense
That gathers honey at her lip shall fool
The resolution and large gravity
That holds my purpose up.   I am no fool ;
I will go through with it ; I am no boy
To be kissed out of mind : I will not fail.   [*Exit.*

   Ca. Yolande, this way ; come nearer, my fair child ;
I love you well ; there 's no such mouth at court
For music and fair color : sit by me ;
How pleasant is it to find eyes to love

That will not cheat or flatter one !   Dear maid,
I think you find a time between two loves
To put some poor dwarfed liking by for me ?
Indeed you may; see if I love you not ;
Get me to proof.

  Yol.   You are my gracious mistress ;
I would be always glad of service done
And found worth taking.

  Ca.   Do you love Denise ?
Meseems the girl grows whiter and less straight,
Dull too, I think ; eh, you think otherwise ?

  Yol. She seems to me grown duller than spoilt wine.

  Ca. I am right glad you do not think her wise.
I have a plan to pleasure mine own self,
And do you good.   Are you content thereto ?

  Yol. Madam, content.

  Ca.   You will not blench away ?
Not lightly start from me ?

  Yol.   I will not so.

  Ca. I trust you perfectly. — Fetch hither to me
That box of mine wherein I keep rare scents ;
You know, the one carved of sweet foreign wood
I use to dress my hair and face withal.

  Yol. Madam, I shall.   *[Exit.*

  Ca.   Ay, it shall do you good.
Will this one hold in wearing ?   I think, yes ;
For I have seen her tread upon sick flies
Where the other swerved, and would not do them hurt.

This Yolande is half cold, and wears her pleasure
No deeper than the skin; thereto she is hard,
Cunning and bold; I have heard tales of her;
She hath the brain and patience of hoar beards
In her most supple body. I do not think
That she shall wry her mouth on tasting blood.

Re-enter YOLANDE.

So, did you miss it?
   Yol.   Madam, it is here.
   Ca. Thanks: have good care of the lid, you see it has
Fair foreign work of cunning little heads
And side-mouthed puppets quaintly cut on it:
See how I pinch it open with a trick;
I would not have all fingers mix in it,
For there are spices which are venomous;
So are best things puddled with ill in them,
We cannot sift them through; nothing so clean
But you may tread it foul, nor so foul anything
That one may never warp its use to good;
As this which puts out men, and is most rare
To sweeten gloves with.
   Yol.   What am I to do?
   Ca. I know not. Set a cushion to my feet;
So. — One has told me each of you to-day
Lay some girl's gift upon that fool of mine:
Is this not true?
   Yol.   Madam, it was our game.

Ca. When you shall see him give him this for me;
　　　　　　　　　(Gives her a glove.)
And yet not me, he loves not me, poor fool;
Say that Denise had wrought him such a glove,
And being incensed at his late insolence
Which he hath put upon the king and her,
Was purposed to withhold it; I will confirm you.
Suppose a shift of mine to vex the fool;
Say what you will, but thrust her name therein;
Look that you take him where she may not see.
Clasp the silk well across my shoulder; thanks;
I am clad too thinly for a queen-mother,
But all this mouth is overhot.   Be sure
Nothing shall stick to us.   Keep close to me.　　　*[Exeunt.*

SCENE II.   *The Admiral's House.*

Enter LA NOUE, TELIGNY, *and* LA ROCHEFOUCAULD.

La N. I fear me he can scantly bear this out.
Tel. Nay, fear him not; there goes more nerve to him
Than to some lesser scores.   His competence
Is like that virtue in his mind which fills
The shallowness of thin occasions up,
And makes him better than the season is
That serves his worth to work in.   He shall not live
And bear himself beyond the fear of time,
Where other men made firm in goodness drop
And are the food of peril.

La R.   Doubtless he is most wise ;
But I misdoubt he doth too much regard
Each trick and shift of bastard circumstance ;
It is the custom and gray note of age
To turn consideration wrong way out
Until it show like fear.
Tel.   I pray, sir, tell me
In what keen matter hath he so blenched aside
Since time began on him ? or in what fashion
Hath he worn fear ?   The man is absolute,
Perfectly tempered ; that I a little speak him,
Your less observance of him shall excuse
And so my praise allow itself.   He hath been
In all hard points of war the best that ever
Did take success by the hand ; the first that wore
Peace as the double coronet of time,
The costly stone set in red gold of war,
So wise to mix reverse with sufferance,
Use fortune with a liberal gravity
And discipline calamitous things with grace,
That failure more approved him, being so shaped
And worn to purpose in his wisdom's worth,
Than men are praised for hazard, though it leaves
Their heads embraced with wealth.   His nobleness of
    speech
Hath made true grace and temperate reserve
But usual names for his ; he is too pure,
Too perfect in all means of exercise

That are best men's best pearl, to be esteemed
At single value of some separate man
That the thin season can oppose to him.

La R. I say not else.

Tel.   So would I have you say.

La R. Had I dispraised the admiral, it had shown
My love to him that I did prick your speech
To such fair estimate of his fair worth.
The man is come.

Enter COLIGNY.

Co.   Good morrow, noble friends.
Fair son, it is a loving bound that doth
Limit your custom thus.

Tel.   I am best pleased
When I may use you thus familiarly.

Co. (*To La R.*) My lord, you told me of a way you had
To bring the matter clear we spoke upon.

La R. Yea, by a woman's means.

Co.   I think it was.

La R. I saw her yesternight.

La N.   You did not say
Where our hopes went? I would not trust you far.

La R. Nay, I did strain discretion out of wear ;
I told her nothing.

Co. ˙   What did you get of her ?
I think you called the woman — umph — Yolande.

La R. That 's your demand, what I did get of her ?
Why, such fair time as women keep for us ;
What better should I get ?

Tel. (*To La N.*)   I fear him greatly;
It is the unwound and ravelled sort of man
That the proof uses worst; so large of lip
Was never yet secure in spirit.
   Co.   Sir,
We have looked for more of you.
   La R.   This is pure truth;
I had such usage as made room for talk,
And in the vantage of occasion put
Inquiry on her, how the queen her mistress
Was moved in temper towards us; did she say thus,
Or thus: you see I spoke not as of purpose
To get this out, but just in some loose way;'
As did she put new color in her hair,
Or what sweet kind of water did she take
To smooth her neck, what powder blanch it with;
And twenty such blown matters out of joint;
Then at the last felt underhand on this,
What were her state-words, her talk's policy;
Which way she bowed; or should the Polish king
Weigh dearer than the duke of Alençon
Or either than this Charles; and thus, and thus;
Being so, you see, bosomed and gathered up
Towards the close and dearest time of all
She could keep nothing safer than her mouth
Would let it out for me; and I as quick
To catch her talk for food as 't were a kiss
The last I thought to find about her lips.

Co. But, to the point she told you of, — if thus
You got one clear.

Tel.   Ay, that, sir, show us that.

La R. Give me the breath to come to it, my lords;
Thus was it; I must hide her foolishness
Deep as trust lies in man; whereon I swore
Ten such sweet oaths as love doth take to wind
His windy weaving up; then she begins
The matter of her fear, thus quakes thereon —

Tel. This will outlive all patience.

La N.   Bear with it.

La R. The queen she said was kind, not given to put
Her care of things outside her talk, but kind,
And would say somewhat — something one might know —
As this; the queen was graciously disposed
And all sick humor of old policies
By this blown out; she would not do men wrong;
We should have music in the month would play
All harsher-throated measures out, and make
Even in the noisy and sick pulse of war   ·
Continual quiet.

Co.   Did she take such words?

La R. Even these I tell you.

Co.   I thank you for their use;
This trouble hath borne fruit to us of yours.

La R. To please a lesser friend than you are, sir,
I 'll undergo worse labor, stretch myself
To a much keener service. Sirs, farewell:

I have a business waits upon the king
That narrows half my leisure seasons in.   [*Exit.*
  Co. What do you say of this ?
  Tel.   May we believe
The Florentine would with so light a key
Lock such deep matter ?   I do not trust the man.
  Co. Sir, what say you ?
  La N.   I rule not by such levels.
  Co. I hold with both of you; and I am glad
The time hath rid him hence.
  Tel.   True, it is fit.
  Co. He weighs much lighter than our counsel may.
By this I doubt not, if his whore spake truth
(As commonly such have repute to trip
At unawares on it, and escape lies
By disesteem of truth) — I say I doubt not
The queen doth something cover in her speech
That has more danger in its likelihood
Than a snake poison.
  La N.   Will you take it so ?
  Co. Nay, so I know it.   Therefore as we prefer
Before the deadly-colored face of war
The cold assurance of a sober peace,
And esteem life beyond death's violence
For all dear friends who hang their weight on us,
It so imports us to make use of time
As never was more need.
  Tel.   What must we do for you ?

    5   G

Co. I would send letters to the province towns
For witness how impaired a state we have
In this loose Paris ; how like beleaguered men
That are at edge' of hunger and begin
To slacken their more temperate advice
And heat the blood of counsel, we are bound
To the service of this danger ; informing further
Of this my hurt, caught unawares at hand
(As proof doth drive beyond the guess) of one
Who wears the gold of Guise at his point's edge
And hath allowance for the use of him
Rightly received.   This being set down, with more
That is but half as hazardous as it
And yet hath face enough, shall sting them through ;
So shall their keener service overcome
The providence of these.

La N.   They shall have news ;
Myself am charged to be from hence this week ;
The office that I have must be my means
To steal upon our friends that lie abroad
And work them to our way.

Tel.   Have you no more ?

Co. This only, that you warn our Paris men
To keep waked eyes this month ; for as I think
(And partly this is gathered of report
Which our late evidence hath put sinew to)
There moves between the Guisards and the queen
Some certain question whose performance will

Bruise us past use. Nay, I am sure of it;
If proof may give security large heart
And things endured be held believable,
Then I am sure. Therefore be wise and swift;
Put iron on your lips, fire in your feet,
And turn trust out of service. I have no more;
For me, this maimed and barren piece I am
May bear the time out, and sufficient roof
Is in the patient cover of a grave
To keep hard weathers off; but for the cause
And for my friends therein I take this care
To counsel you. Farewell.

Tel., La N.   Farewell, great lord.

> [*Exeunt severally.*

SCENE III.   *The Louvre.*

Enter the Queen-Mother, MARGARET, DENISE, YOLANDE,
and other Ladies.

Ca. Call in my fool. You have all made proof of love
Except Denise; nay, she shall gift him too.
I prithee call him to us. (*Exit* DENISE.) And yet I think
The fellow turns half sour about the lip,
Being almost wholly dull.

Mar.   Nay, I keep friends with him.

Ca. That 's like enough, for he doth love your husband.
But the lewd words he put upon my son
And on Denise, did all but quite condemn

Our meek account of them.   It is no matter,
If she can pardon him.

Re-enter DENISE *with* CINO.

O, sir, come hither.
Cino. I shall run at your bidding, shall I not?
Ca. What should you do?
Mar.   Ay, there, what would you be?
Cino. Not fool enough to be a dog of yours.
Mar. This is no fool; he can do naught but rail.
Yol. The fool has strayed among the gospellers.
Cino. I begin to see I am virtuous; the wicked abuse
    me.
Ca. Come hither, sirrah.   Look well upon this fellow;
Would you not say a fool so round of flesh
'Should be as courteous as a spaniel, ha?
Make answer, sir; we are told news of you,
What licensed things inhabit in your lip
That should be whipt ere heard, corrected first
And after to offend : what say you to 't?
Cino. Now shall I slip for want of a good tongue
And have my patience beaten.   Prithee lend me
A tongue of yours.
Ca.   Have I more tongues than one?
Cino. A score or so.
Ca.   Show us a little first
What sort of speech thy mother taught thee mar.
Mar. Ay, there it lies; try that.

Cino.   What will you have me say?

Yol. His jests are waste.

Anne.   Pure scandal screams in them.

Cino. You call me gospeller, ha?

Yol.   Nay, that did I.

Cino. Shall I turn preacher for your sake and make
A parable of your mouths?

Mar.   That, that; come on.

Yol. Put your worst wrath on us.

Renée.   We 'll hear the fool.

Anne. Speak large and open; spare us not; speak
   wide.

Yol. Now the mill grinds; now mark.

Cino.   But I shall rail indeed
Now I have holy leave.

Mar.   No matter; prithee now.

Cino. It is your preacher's parable and not mine
Who am your poor fool and a simple thing.

Ca. Come, sir, dig out your spleen.

Cino.   Thus then. You are all goats —

Mar. Ha?

Ca.   Hear him through; we must have lewder stuff.

Cino. And that which should make humbled blood in
   you
And clothe your broader times with modesty
Runs all to spoil and plagues your veins with heat.

Yol. We must have more.

Anne.   This is blunt matter, fool.

Cino. Hunger abides in you as in a dog
That has been scanted of flesh-meat three days ;
Sin doth make house with you.   Are you pleased yet ?
You have smooth Sodom in your shameful cheeks ;
Respect, obedience, the shut lips of fear,
Worship and grace and observation,
You have not heard of more than spring-swoln kine
Have heard of temperance.   Are you yet satisfied ?
    Ca. This is dead ware.
    Mar.   Mere chaff that chokes the bin.
    Yol. The dust of a fool's bones.
    Anne.   Dull as a preacher's beard.
    Cino. But are you not ? resolve me ; are not you ?
You are made up of stolen scraps of man
That were filched unawares ; you can make no children
Because you are grown half male with wicked use.
    Ca. I 'll have thee whipt ; thou art a hollow fool,
And hast no core but pith.   Why, any beast
That hath the spring of speech in his tongue's joint
Or any talking nerve, could breed to this.
Thou wert to make us mirth.
    Cino.   Well, do I not ? do I not ?
    Mar. Who angles in thee save for weeds, shall trip
Over his ears in mire : shut thy lewd mouth.
    Ca. Will you take gifts to be dumb ? we are wearied
        with you.
    Cino. Ay, and worse favors at your prayer I will.
    Ca. You look near white with laughing much, Yolande ;

Nay, there 's no need to catch so sharp at red.
Give me that glove you keep for him.
  Yol.   Here, madam.
  Ca. Here, wear this, Cino, and be friends with us.
  Cino. A fair gold thing, a finch's color i' the back ;
Too small for me though ; God change one of us.
  Ca. Denise gave me the glove.
  Den.   I, gracious madam ?
  Ca. You, gracious maiden ; it would span your wrist.
So, fool ; beware you do not rend it.
  Yol.   Ah !
  Ca. What now ? did a gnat sting you ?
  Yol.   A mere fly ;
A mere gold fly ; I took it for a wasp.
  Mar. What does this mean ? Come hither, fool ; sit
  here.
  Ca. I will not have him there. — Stand farther off. —
The knave's report doth poison miles about ;
Come half so close, he 'll kill you in your ear.
  Cino. Have back your glove ; here, madam, have it
  back ;
I will not wear it.
  Mar.   What stings him now i' the brain ?
  Cino. I am not well.
  Ca.   This is some sideways jest.
  Den. (*Aside.*) God make this business better than my
  thought,
For I do fear it.

Mar.   Do you note his lips?

Yol. Yea, his eyes too?

Anne.   He is not well indeed.

Was all his railing prologue to this play

That reads as dull as death?

Cino.   Now I could prophesy

Like who turns heaven to riddles; my brain beats.

A man were as good ask mercy of dead bones

As of the best lip here; nay, I shall be

Quite marred amongst you.

Ca.   Convey the fool from us;

This does not look like wine.

Cino. God be with you; be wise now, for the fool is

    gone.   [*Exit.*

Ca. I do not like the face of this. Where had you

The glove you gave me?

Den.   I gave you nothing, madam.

Ca. Does that wind hold? I must have more of you.

Mar. Madam, you do not think —

Ca.   Give me leave, sweet.

We have had too much peril in report

To let this lie so light. Where had you it?

Den. Why do you bait me out of season thus?

You know I never had it.

Ca.   Oh! had you not?

Then I have dreamed awry of you.

Den.   Madam —

        Enter Attendant.

Att. Where is the queen ?

Ca.   What puts such haste in you ?   ,

Am I not worth a knee ?

Att.   Pardon me, madam,

I have such tidings ; your poor fool is dead.

Ca. Bring me to him. So suddenly to cease

Is to cry out on his death's manner ; bring me

To see his body ; I have a little craft

In such a matter's healing. Some of you

Look to that girl ; she swoons to have the deed

So entered in her ears.

Mar.   It is too foul.

Ca. God pardon her ! Could she not see that sharpness

Was but the gall and flaw of his bowed brain ?

It did not hurt her more, being most proclaimed,

Than she has pitied him. Bring her with us.

                                        [*Exeunt.*

5*

ACT IV.

SCENE I. *The Louvre.*

Enter LA NOUE, SOUBISE, *and* PARDAILLAN.

Pardaillan.

I HAVE not heard such news.

La N.   'Faith, they sound ill;
If women of so choice and costly names
Turn worse than popular murders are, we have all
Much need to help ourselves.

Sou.   This is their fashion;
Their blood is apt to heats so mutable
As in their softer bodies overgrow
The temper of sweet reason, and confound
All order but their blood.

Par.   You read them well;
Good reason have you to put reason to 't
And measure them by the just line of it.

La N. But that such sins should plague the feverish
    time
I do not wonder far; all things are grown .
Into a rankness.

Par.   Still I say, a woman
To do such bitter deeds —

Sou.   That 's where it sticks.

Par. Put on such iron means —

Sou.   Ay, that, sir, that.

Par. So rip the garments of their temperance

And keep no modest thing about their face

To hide the sin thereon : pluck off the shows

That did o'erblanch a little —   .

Sou.   Ay, keep there.

La N. But, gentlemen, what upshot hear you of?

Par. The queen hath sent her under heavy guard

To bide some subtler edge of evidence

Here in her chamber.

Sou.   Why not in prison?

Look you, they 'll let her slip ; I say they will.

Par. But hear you, sir ; I did not blame the queen —

Sou. It doth outgrow the height and top of shame

That she should pass untaxed.

Par.   She will not pass.

Sou. Take note, sir, there is composition in 't :

They would not put imprisonment on her ;

Why this is rank : I tell you this is rank.

Par. God's pity ! what a perfect wasp are you !

Why, say she scapes — as by my faith I see

No such keen reason why she should not scape,

The matter being so bare and thin in proof

As it appears by this —

La N.   Yea, so I say ;

If she be manifest a murderess —

Sou.   If !

What "if" will serve? show me the room for "if";
I read no reason on the face of "if."
If she be not, what leans our faith upon?
If she be pure or only possible
For judgment to wash clear, — if she be not
Evident in guilt beyond all evidence, —
The perfect map where such red lines are drawn
As set down murder, — if she be less one whit
I 'll take her sin upon myself and turn
Her warrant.

    Par.   Take a woman's sin on you?
O, while you live, lay no such weight on faith,
'T will break her back. Sir, as you love me, do not;
I would not have you take such charge upon you.

    Sou. I say I will not; for I can approve
Her very guiltiness.

    Par.   Nay, that clears all.
But it is strange that one so well reputed,
So perfect in all gentle ways of time
That take men's eyes — in whom the slips she had
Were her more grace and did increase report
To do her good — who might excuse all blame
That the tongued story of this time could lay
On her most sweet account, — that such a lady
Should wreak herself so bloodily for words
Upon a shallow and sick-witted fool.
Why, what is she the better, he removed?
Or how doth he impair her, being alive?
There 's matter in 't we know not of.

Sou. Yea, why?
For that you speak of her repute, my lord,
I am not perfect in a girl's repute ;
It may be other than I think of it;
But in this poor conjectural mind of mine
I cannot see how to live large and loose
Doth put a sounder nerve into repute
Than honest women have. What we did know of her,
You, I, and all men —
   Par. Nay, you tax her far.
Sou. I mean, we know her commerce with the king ;
Ha? did we not?
   Par. Yea, that was broad enough.
Sou. Why, well then, how doth she make up repute,
Being patched so palpably? Here comes the queen.

Enter the King, *the* Queen-Mother, *and* LA ROCHEFOUCAULD.

   Ch. It may be so.
   Ca. I would it had less face.
If likelihood could better speak of her,
I should be glad to help it.
   Sou. Marked you this?
   Ca. But shame can hide no shame so manifest ;
It must all out.
   Ch. I do not say it must.
   Ca. Why, it was open, proof doth handle it ;
The poor brain-bitten railer chid at her,
Scoffed in lewd words, made speech insufferable

Of any temperate ear ; no colder cheek
But would have burnt at him ; myself was angered,
Could not wear patience through ; and she being quick,
Tendering her state as women do, too slight
To push her reason past her anger's bound —

Sou. Did you note that ? she speaks my proper way.

Ca. She being such doth with my hands resolve
To whip him out of life ; and in this humor —

Ch. Soft now ; I must get proof ; what makes your highness
In such a matter ?

Ca.   I gave her glove to him.

Ch. O, this is well ; and yet she murdered him ?

Par. What says your judgment to 't ? have you no quirk ? (*Aside.*)

Ca. She gave it me ; I had the glove of her.

Par. Does the wind blow that side ?

Sou.   Notice the king ; he chafes.

[*Exeunt* PARDAILLAN, SOUBISE, *and* LA NOUE.

Ch. Our sister says she did outswear you all
She never saw the glove.

Ca.   Put her to proof ;
Let her outbrag by evidence evidence,
And proof unseat by proof.

Ch.   Call her to me.

Ca. That were unfit ; you shall not see her.

Ch.   Shall not !
Who puts the "shall not" on me ? is it you ?

Ca. Not I, but absolute need and present law;
She is not well; and till she be made whole
There shall no trial pass upon her proof;
She shall have justice; it may be she is clear,
And this large outward likelihood may lie;
Then she were sharply wronged; and in that fear
And also for dear love I bear to her
I have removed her with no care but mine
To a more quiet room; where till more surety
She doth abide in an unwounded peace,
Having most tender guard.

Ch.   I 'll write her comfort;
For I do know she has much wrong in this.

Ca. I will commend you verbally to her;
The other were some scandal.

Ch.   Pray you, do;
Look you speak gently; I would not have you loud,
For she will weep all pity into you
To see her cheek so marred. Look you say well;
Say I do nothing fear but she is wronged,
And will do right; yea, though I loved her not
(As truly I am not so hard in love
But I can see her fault, which is much pity, —
A very talking error in weak tongues)
I would not have her wronged. Look you say that.

Ca. I will say anything.

Ch.   Now, my fair lord,
Have I done well?

La R.   Most justly and most well.

Ch. You would not else, were you a king of mine ?

La R. I would do this, even merely as you do.

Ch. What say you to this evidence ?

La R.   That it doth

Amaze my sense of what is proven ; for,

If there be witness in the touch and grasp

Of things so palpable, and naked likelihood

Outpoises all thin guess and accident,

I must believe what makes belief rebel

And turn a proclaimed liar.   For I am sure

That she whose mouth this proof doth dwell upon,

I mean the virtuous damozel Yolande,

Is past the tax of lying ; she is as pure

As truth desires a man.

Ch.   It is most strange ;

Let's find some smoother talk.   Have you not seen

My book of deer, what seasons and what ways

To take them in ?   I finished it last night.

La R. I have not seen it.

Ch.   Only this throws me out ;

(The verses, Peter Ronsard made them rhyme)

I'll show you where ; come, you shall get me through ;

You are perfect at such points.

La R.   Your praise outruns me.

Ch No, not a whit ; you are perfect in them ; come.

                    [*Exeunt* King *and* La Rochefoucauld.

Ca. This is the proper cooling of hot blood ;

Now is she lost in him. Say, she doth live; to put
Earth in her lips and dusty obstacle
May not be worth my pains. She cannot thwart me either;
For say I did enfranchise her to-night,
Give air and breath to her loud'st speech, she could not
Wrench one man's faith awry. Yet since I know
Security doth overlean itself
And bruise its proper side, I will not do 't.
Or say I win her back; and being so won,
I may find serviceable times for her
To spy upon king fool; this coolness thawed
Would make a heat indeed. There 's use for her
And room withal; if she leave tenderness
And this girl's habit of a changing blood,
I can as well unload her of this weight
As I did lay it on; which being kept up
May make her life bend under it, and crack
The sensible springs of motion. I will put proof to it;
Favor of love, promise and sweet regard,
Large habit, and the royal use of time,
May her slight fear as potently outpoise
As wisdom doth, weighed in a steadier brain.   [*Exit.*

SCENE II. *Denise's Apartment in the same.*

Enter DENISE *and* Attendant.

Att. How do you now?

Den.   Well; I do ever well;
It comes not new to me, this well-doing.

H

I sleep as women do that feed well, I feed
As those who wear the gold of doing well.
What pricks you so to ask? Why, this is quaint,
I cannot brace my body like a maid's,
Cannot plait up my hair, gather a pin,
But you must catch me with "How do you it?"

 Att. I made but question of that mood you had
Some three hours back, when you fell pale and wept,
Saying fever clenched you fast and you would die;
That mood forgets you.

 Den.   Not a whit; you slip
Strangely between conjectures of two sides,
The white and black side. I am very well.
They say "do well" if one does virtuously;
May I not say so?

 Att.   Doubtless you may well.

 Den. Yea, the word "well" is tied upon your tongue.
Try now some new word, prithee some fair phrase,
Rounder i' the mouth than "well"; I hate this "well";
I pray you learn some lesson of a jay
To use new words. I will provide me one
That shall say nothing all day through but "ill,"
And "ill" again. I 'll have a clock tick "well"
And hang it by your bed to wake you mad
Because you chatter me half sick with "well."

 Att. I will say nothing lest you carp at me,
Planting offence in most pure sentences;
Mistake falls easy.

Den. Truly it doth fall.
All matters fall out somehow in God's work,
And round the squaréd edges of them flat.
But I fall wrong, slip someway short of heaven,
And earth fails too, and leaves me dismal hell,
Naked as brown feet of unburied men.
Think you they hold mere talk like ours in hell?
Go up and down with wretched shoulders stooped
And wried backs under the strong burdens bruised
And thwarted bodies without pleasant breath?

Att. I do conceive it as clean fire that burns
And makes a gray speck of the gracious corn;
God keep us that we burn not in such wise.

Den. That is a prayer, and prayers are sweet. But then
We 'll have no praying; only such as this, —
I prithee set a finger to my load,
Help me from fainting; take my knife and smite
And put the blood to cool upon my mouth.
Such dull work too as carls get sickened with
And turn to die into the black rank straw,
We shall set hands to; all fair lords and knights,
Great kings with gold work wrought into their hair,
Strong men of price and such as play or sing,
Delicate ladies with well-shodden feet,
Tall queens in silk wear and all royal things,
Yea, priests of noble scarlet and chaste mark,
All shall God set awork. Peradventure too
When our arms loosen in the elbow-joints

With the strong rage and violent use of toil,
He may send patient breath to ease our lips
And heal us for a little weeping-space,
But then in talking each with each will grow
Worse shame and wholly fashioned wretchedness,
And either will go back to mere short moans
And the hard pulse of his outlabored hour
Rather than talk.   We shall lie down and curse
Stupidly under breath, like herdsmen ; turn
And hide and cover from all witness up,
Each his own loathing and particular sore ;
Sit with chins fallen and lank feet asquat,
Letting the dismal head work its own way,
Till the new stripe shall pluck us up to task,
Crossing with cruelties our own bad will,
Crowning our worst with some completed bad
Too ill to face.   Ay, this should be their way ;
For fire and all tormented things of earth
Are parcels of good life, have use and will,
Learn worthiest office and supply brave wants ;
And not the things that burn up clean make hell,
Not pain, hate, evil, actual shame or sense,
But just the lewd obedience, the dead work,
The beaten service of a barren wage
That gets no reaping.

    Att. I cannot taste the purpose of your speech.
Pray you lie down.

    Den.   I will not. Well it were

To set our upper lives on some such guise
And have a perfect record when one dies
How things shall be thereafter. A knowledge armed
Of the most sharp and outermost event
Is half a comfort. I do think for one
That God will set me into certain hell,
Pick me to burn forth of his yellow spears
Like any tare as rank. Also I doubt
There shall be some I had to do withal
Packed in the same red sheaf. How will each look,
Tavannes, no leaner than the hound he was,
Or Guise beard-singed to the roots ? the queen-mother
Tied by the hair to — I get idle now.
A grave thing is it to feel sure of hell,
But who should fear it if I slip the chance
And make some holy blunder in my end,
Translating sin by penitence ? For none
Sinned ever yet my way ; treason and lust
Sick apes, red murder a familiar fool,
To this new trick set by them, will be shamed
In me forever ; yea, contempt of men
Shall put them out of office. He that lusts,
Envies, or stabs, shall merely virtuous be,
And the lank liar fingering at your throat
A friend right honest. That roadway villain's knife
That feels for gold i' the womb, shall be not hated ;
And the cold thief who spills a popular breath
Find grace o' the gallows ; why do men hang poor knaves,

Cut throats while mine goes smooth ?   Now I think on 't,
I will put condemnation to their act
By mine own will and work.   I pray you kill me,
I will not hurt you.
    Att.   Alas, she is mad.   Dear lady —
    Den. Yea, dear; I shall be dear some three days hence,
And paid full price.   Dost thou not think I am mad ?
I am not; they would fain have lied me mad,
Burnt up my brain and strung my sense awry,
In so vile space imprisoning my wants
I can help nothing.   Here sit I now, beast-like,
Loathsomely silenced : who, if I had the tongue
Wherewith hard winter warns the unblanched sea,
Would even outspeak the winds with large report,
Proclaming peril.   But being this I am
I get no help at all.   One maimed and dumb
That sees his house burn, such am I.   My God !
Were it not sweeter to be finished well
Than still hold play with hangman anger?

                Enter the Queen-Mother.

    Ca.   Leave us, girl.   [*Exit* Attendant.
Nay, sit; this reverence hath no seed in you;
Sit still.
    Den.   Madam —
    Ca.   Good lady, will you sit ?
    Den. So you be come to bind more shame on me,
I can well bear more shame.

Ca.   You are still foolish;
How have I set this anger in your face?
I make no parcel of these tears of yours;
No word that gets upon your lips to weep
Have I given use for.

Den.   Ay, no use you say?
But I dream not that hold this hand in that,
But I dream not that take your eyes with mine;
But I dream not I am that very thing
That as a taint inside the imperilled flesh
Have made corruption of the king's close will,
Put scarlet treason on his purpose, marred
The face of confidence, plucked words from trust,
Taught murder to walk smooth and set his feet
Upon the ways of faith; I am that thing,
I would it were some other.

Ca.   Have you yet done?

Den. Yea, I have done all this.

Ca.   I do believe you;
And though your thoughts ungently look my way,
I have such sorrow for you sown at heart
As you should reap a liberal help thereof
Would you but pay thin thanks.

Den.   No, I'll no thanks;
Yea, though I die, I will not thank you; no;
For I can hold my breath into my lip,
Or twist my hair to choke my throat upon,
Or thrust a weak way thus to my rent heart

Even with these bare and feeble fingers here,
Making each nail a knife ; look you, I 'll do 't.
   Ca. You talk too wide ; I came to do you good.
   Den. That were good news indeed ; things new, being
     good,
Come keener to put relish in the lip ;
I pray you let me see this good i' the face,
Look in its eyes to find dead colors out,
For deadly matters make up good for me.
   Ca. Nay, you shall find my favor large as love ;
I make no talk of gold, no costly words,
No promise, but this merely will I say,
You holding by me grapple to a hold
Full of all gracious office and such wealth
As love doth use for surety ; such good riches
As on these latter lips of womanhood
Are sweet as early kisses of a mouth
Scented like honey. Keep but fast my side,
No time shall hew the planted root away
That faith of your dear service sets in me,
Nor violence of mistempered accident
Cleave it across.
   Den.   I would I were clear of you.
What would you get ? You are a great queen, grave soul,
Crown-shaped i' the head ; your work is wonderful
And stoops men to you by the neck, but I
Can scantly read it out. I know just this, —
Take you this patience from my wretched lips,

Pluck off this evidence of the bolted steel,
Make wide the passage of my chambered feet
And I will take a witness in my mouth
To set the cries of all the world on you
And break my shame to lead your neck with half
Like a thief's neck.

    Ca.   You are slower than weighed lead
To use my speech aright. But though you be
Twice dull or thrice, and looser of your lip
Than that swift breath that outwings rumor, yet
No babble slipt upon my purposes
Could manage me a peril, no tongue's trip
Cross me between. Who puts belief to speech
Grown from some theft, that stains me with report
From mine own lips caught like infection ? Look,
Though you could preach my least word spoken out
To the square in Paris where noise thickens most,
It hurts me nothing. 'T is not that populous tongue
That savors insolence and raw distaste
Can riot out my will. Nay, keep your cheeks :
I would not kill the color past all help,
For I have care of you ; and liberal fruit
Shall you reap of it, and eat quiet bread
When white want shrinks the rest.

    Den.   I will not do it.
Nay, though I were your foolish workwoman,
There is no room for good to do me good ;
That blessed place wherein love kissed me first

6

Is now waxed bare enough.   I might ask alms
Of meanest men, being by mine own repute
Made less than time makes them; I am not good nor fair,
For the good made on me by love is gone,
And that affection of the flattered blood
Which fills this holy raiment of the soul
With inwrought shapeliness and outside rose
Keeps now no tide in me; the unpulsed sense
Hath like a water settled and gets flat
As dead sands be at utmost ebb that drink
The drainéd salt o' the sea.   Nay, to talk thus
Is foolish as large words let out in drink;
Therefore I am not wise ; what would you have of me?
  Ca.   Nay, nothing but your peace, which I 'll assure
Beyond large time's assault.   Yet I 'll do something with
     you,
Put sudden bitter in your sweet of lips,
A knife's edge next your throat, that when you drink
Shall spill out wine i' the blood, — something like this;
Feed you upon the doubt, and gnash and grieve,
Feeling so trapped.   You 'll show fierce teeth at me,
Take threats of me into your milky mouth?
You 'll maim my ruined patience, put me out
Of sober words and use of gravities?
  Den.   Yea, I can read you are full-tempered now;
But your sharp humors come not in my fear.
  Ca.   Yea so ? high-tempered said she ? yea, true, true, —
I 'm angered, — give me water to cool out

This o'er-tongued fever of intemperance.
Bid one come in and see how wroth I am;
Am I not angered now? see you, — and you, —
Do not I chafe and froth the snaffle white
With the anger in my mouth? see, do I not?
— Thou hast the tender impotence of talk
That men teach daws; a pitiful thing, — in sooth
I am not so chafed; I have something in my will
That makes me chide at thee, my plaything; look,
I do half choose to chide at it, sweet wretch,
It almost chafes me such a daw should live.

   Den. It chafes me too; I will not be forgiven;
If shame go smooth and blood so supple it,
Kingdoms will turn from the grave word of man
To side with hoofèd herds: I were best die
And get no grace of God.

   Ca.   "No grace" it said?
Dost thou make such a gracious dunce of God
To look thee out in the time's jarring sum,
Choose thy room forth and hearken after thee
To find thee place and surety and eased breath?
God's no such bat to be at pains for this.
Pray now, go pray; speak some wise word or two
To pluck his mercies back your way. God's name!
It marvels me how any fool i' the flesh
Must needs be sure of some fore-facing help
To make him fragrant means for living well,
Some blind God's favor bound across his head

To stamp him safe i' the world's imperilling.
Pardon thy sin ? who blabs thy pretty slips
I' the ear of his broad knowledge, scores thy stains,
Makes him partaker of all times and rooms
Where thou hast made shuddering occasions
To try Eve's huskless apple with thy teeth ?
Doth such care dwell on thy breath's lean reserves,
Thy little touches and red points of shame ?
I tell thee, God is wise and thou twice fool,
That wouldst have God con thee by rote, and lay
This charge on thee, shift off that other charge,
And mete thine inward inches out by rule
That hath the measure of sphered worlds in it
And limit of great stars.   Wilt thou serve yet ?

  Den. Not you herein at all ; though you spake right.
As it may be this speech does call truth kin,
I would not sin beyond my ancient way
And couple with new shame.

    Ca.   This is your last ;
For the sad fruit that burgeons out of this
Take your own blame, for I will none. — You, there,
You that make under uses of the door,
Leave off your ear-work and come in ; nay, come ;

            Enter YOLANDE.

Here 's use for you ; look well upon this girl,
Count well the tender feet that make her flesh
And her soft inches up ; nay, view them close ;
For each poor part and specialty of her

You hold sharp count to me ; I 'll have you wise ;
You that are portress shall be jailer — you,
Mark me, just you —⁣ I would not have you slip ;
Come not into my danger ; but keep safe,
I do you good indeed.

Yol.   I will do truly.

Ca. Farewell, sweet friend ; (*to Denise*) I am right
    grieved that you
Will mix my love with your impatience.
Though I more thinly fare in your esteem,
Fare you yet well for mine, and think of me
More graciously than thus ; so have you peace
As I do wish you happily to have.
God give you sleep. — Look heedfully to her
As you would have me prosperous to you. [*Exeunt severally.*

SCENE III.   *The Marshal's House.*

Enter two Captains.

1 *Cap.* May this be true that we are bidden so ?
2 *Cap.* I think it is.
1 *Cap.*   Did the king speak with you ?
1 *Cap.* No, the lord marshal.
  1 *Cap.*   He is hot on this ;
But did he tell you to be forth to-night ?
2 *Cap.* Before the chime of twelve.
1 *Cap.*   Why then we have
A broken four hours' work upon us yet

Between this time and that most bloody one.
There is a yellow point upon the sky
Where the last upper sun burns sideways out,
Scoring the west beneath.

  2 *Cap.*   I see the mark:
It shines against the Louvre ; it is nigh gone.

  1 *Cap.* Yea, the strong sun grows sick ; but not to
    death.   ˋ
Which side have you to take ?

  2 *Cap.*   ·   The south side, I.

  1 *Cap.* I to the west. Would this were really through.

  2 *Cap.* Who gave you news o' the office ?

  1 *Cap.*   Maurevel.

  2 *Cap.* O, he that hurt the admiral some days back ?
That plague-botch of the Guisards ?

  1 *Cap.*   Yea, the same:
I had a mind to strike him in the mouth.

  2 *Cap.* Why had you so ? you have the better place.

  1 *Cap.* O, sir, in such hard matters he does best
Who does not most. I had rather be a dog,
One half unleashed to feed on bitten orts
Than have his post herein.

  2 *Cap.*   Whose ? Maurevel's ?

  1 *Cap.* Even his ; for he has carved him a broad piece
Out of the body of this wounded town.

  2 *Cap.* What, does the work so startle you ? for me,
I hold it light as kissing a girl's head.

  1 *Cap.* If they should face us, well ; but to put knives
Into their peaceable and sleeping beds —

2 *Cap.* You talk too like a fool.   I loathe so far
Their slow lank ways of envious gravity,
Their sparing pride and lavish modesty,
Cunning so tempered with hot insolence
As in that Pardaillan — in him or him —
I say·I do abhor them, and in my soul
I think there 's no priest half so glad as I
To rid them out of wrong doing.   We are
Most kind to them ; for give their sin more space,
Each year should heap up hell upon their backs
And leave them hotter ; whereas we rid them now
And they just die half-damned.
    1 *Cap.*   You are merciful.
    2 *Cap.* I would be so ; for him whose spleen is thick,
Made bitter and side-clogged with cruel use,
I hate as much as these.
    1 *Cap.*   The marshal tarries ;
I doubt there will be nothing done.
    2 *Cap.*   You doubt ?
Say you desire it ; if you pray for it,
Shame not to answer your own hope.
    1 *Cap.*   I do not ;
I should be glad if all went out in speech
And never smutched our hands with smoke thereof.
    2 *Cap.* This is your poor and barren piety
That mercy calls offence, and law doth put
Rebuke upon.   I do not praise it in you.
    1 *Cap.* Do you mislike it ?

2 *Cap.*   If I should say I did —

1 *Cap.* What then ?

2 *Cap.*   I did you nothing less than right.

1 *Cap.* You will not say so.

2 *Cap.*   By your head, I do ;
I will and do.

1 *Cap.*   This will take time to mend.

2 *Cap.* Mend it your way ; take time to patch it with ;
My hand shall not be slack. Here comes the marshal.

Enter TAVANNES.

Tav. Now, sirs, how are your men disposed ? have you
Had pains with them ?

1 *Cap.*   Mine gave no pains at all.

Tav. Why, well ; I would the temper of such men
Were made the habit of all France. Sir, yours ?

2 *Cap.* I may say better of them ; I could not
So eagerly give tongue to my desire
But they did grasp it first ; such emulous haste
To jostle speech aside with the push of act
I have not known.

Tav.   Good ; they do hunger, then ?

2 *Cap.* Sir, most impatiently.

Tav.   Their galls are hot ?

2 *Cap.* Enough to burn out patience from the world.

Tav. Such I would have ; good dogs, keen in the feet,
Swoln in the spleens of them ; 't is very good.
Your presence flags, sir.

1 *Cap.* Mine, my lord?

Tav. Ay, sir.
You have the gait of an unmaidened girl
That carries violence in her girdle.   Humph!
I do not relish it.

1 *Cap.* My lord —

Tav. Ay, what?
Speak your own way; make answer; nay, be swift.

1 *Cap.* My lord, you have not known me blink or blench
In the red face of death; no peril hath
Put fear upon my flesh, altered the heat
That colors on my cheek the common blood
To a dead sickness or a bruise of white;
Nor doth it now.

Tav. No, doth not? are you sure?

1 *Cap.* You do not think so.

Tav. Nay, there's no peril in 't.
But you had more; make out the worst; get on.

1 *Cap.* Truly I have a motion in my blood
Forbidding such a matter to receive
Smooth entertainment there; I would be fain
To shift the service off; my fellow here
Knows I regard it something loathfully.

Tav. Ay, do you, sir?

2 *Cap.* Indeed he said so.

Tav. Said?

2 *Cap.* But I do know him for a noble man
That would acknowledge all things honorably,

6*

I

Commune with no base words, nor wear such office
As cowards do; I must report him such.

Tav You must! I pray show me what humor then
Crosses him thus at point.

2 *Cap.*   I will not think.

Tav. Sir, you that have such tender make at heart,
That wear a woman in your blood, and put
Your mother on your cheeks, — you that are pure,
That will not fail, — you piece of dainty talk, —
Pluck me this halting passion from your heart,
Or death shall nail it there.

1 *Cap.*   I do not fear you, sir.

Tav. Observe me, sir; I do not use to threat;
Either take up your office for this time
And use it honorably, or I will leave you
No place at all. What sort of fool are you
To start at such a piece of lawful work
As is the manage of more noble hands
Than are familiar with your beard? You are
Too gross a fool.

1 *Cap.*   My lord, you wrong me much.

2 *Cap.* Sir, you push far; he is a gentleman.

Tav. The Devil shall make a better of strawn dung;
I do proclaim him for a thief, a coward,
A common beggar of safe corner-holes,
A chamber hireling to wash pots — Begone,
I will not bear such knaves. Take you his place.
Go, go, eat scraps.

1 *Cap.*   Sir, you shall do me right.

Tav. I say thou art a knave, a side-stair thief, —

God's precious body! I am sick with anger

That such a pad of slack worm-eaten silk

Should wear the name of any soldiership.

Give up thine office.

1 *Cap.*   You do yourself much shame. [*Exit.*

Tav. Fie on him, rag! frayed velvet face! I'd beat him   .

But for pure shame. So, is he gone? Make after

And push him out at door. Take you his place.

Attend me presently.

2 *Cap.*   My lord, I shall.   [*Exeunt.*

SCENE IV. *The Louvre.*

The Queen-Mother, MARGARET, Duchess of Lorraine, *and
Ladies.*

Ca. No, no, the scandal stands with us, not you

That have no lot in it. Well, God be praised,

It does not touch me inwardly and sharp

To be so rid of him; but I do pity

The means of his removal, from my heart

I pity that. 'T is a strange deed; I have not

Seen any that may call it brother, since

That dame's who slew her lord, being caught in middle

Of some more lewd delight; her name now?

Duch.   Châteaudun.

Ca. True, so it was; I thank you; Châteaudun.

Mar. How says she yet? will she confess his death?

Ca. No, but outbears all comfort with keen words.

Mar. Truth, I commend her for it; I would not have
        her
Show the wet penitence of fools that are
More weak than what they do.

Ca.   I partly hold with you.
Have we no music? Nay, I would hear none;
I am not bowed that way; my sense will not stoop
To the pleasurable use of anything.
Is it not late?

Mar.   I think it wears to nine.

Ca. Nay, it lies further; I am sure it does.

Duch. Madam, it is not late.

Ca.   I say it is;
If I am pleased to reckon more than you,
It shall be late.

Mar.   I promised at this time
To be about my husband; if I fail,
My faith is breached with flaw of modesty.

Duch. Nay, go not yet.

Ca.   Will you lay hands on her?

Duch. I do beseech you —

Mar.   What makes you cling to that?

Duch. If you would show me kindness, do not go.

Ca. You play love's fool awry.

Mar.   Show me some reason.

Duch. I have no reason broader than my love;

And from the sweetest part of that sweet love
I do entreat you that you will not go,
But wake with me to-night. I am not well.
 Mar. Sister, I am quite lost in your desire.
 Ca. What, are you ill? how shall it get you whole
To wake the iron watches of the night
Companioned with hard ache of weariness
And bitter moods that pain feeds full upon?
Come, you are idle; I will wake with you,
If you must wake; trouble not her so much.
 Mar. Indeed it would a little tax me.
 Ca.   Nay,
Think not upon it; get you hence and sleep.
Commend me to your lord; bid him thank me
That he to-night doth side you; it is a grace
Worth honorable thanks.
 Duch.   Still I beseech you
To keep me company some poor two hours;
My prayer is slight, more large my need of it;
I charge you for pure pity stay with me.
 Ca. Are you gone mad? what makes your prayer in
  this?
As you regard my wrath or my fair mood,
And love me better peaceable than harsh,
Make a quick end of words. — Margaret, good night. —
Nay, sit you close. — At once good night, my love;
I pray you do my message.
 Mar.   Madam, I will;

No less fair night with you and with my sister,
Whom I shall look to see as whole in health
As sound in spirit.

Ca.   I will take pains for it;
She shall get healed with pains; have no such fear.

[*Exit* MARGARET.

Are you so much a fool? by heaven, I am ashamed
That ever I did use your faith like mine,
Nay that some blood of mine was lost on you
To make such shallow stuff as you are of.

Duch. Madam, you have not thought —

Ca.   What ailed my wits
To lay so precious office on your brain,
Which is filled out with female matters, marred
With milky mixtures? I do loathe such women
Worse than a leper's mouth.

Duch.   Consider but her state ·
It is your flesh, my sister and my blood,
That must look death in the eyes; you bid her hold
Keen danger by the skirt, gripe hands with him; ·
For those that scape the edges of your men,
Being refuged in her lodging, may as well
Turn their own points on her; if none escape,
Then in the slaying of her husband's men
She may well chance on some one's iron side
And death mistake her end.

Ca.   I did mistake
More grossly, to believe the blood in you

Was not so mean in humor as it is.
She is safe enough ; he that but strikes at her
With his bare hand doth pluck on his bare head
Sudden destruction. Say she were not safe,
Must we go back for that and miss the way
That we have painfully carved out and hewn
From the most solid rivet of strong time ?
   Duch. If you would bid her watch —
   Ca.   I will do nothing.
   Duch. Let me but speak to her.
   Ca.   You shall not move ;
This thing is heavier than you think of it
And has more cost than yours. You shall sit still,
And shall not frown or gape or wag your head,
As you respect the mood of my misliking.

Enter Attendant.

   Att. Madam, the Duke of Anjou —
   Ca.   What would he ?
   Att. He prays you dearly be about the king ;
What he would have I cannot tell ; I am sure
He is much moved, and, as I think, with fear.
   Ca. This is an absolute summons. I will go.
                     [Exit Attendant.
So, get you in ; you have no lot beyond ;
That I should have such need to use such fools !
Get you to bed and sleep.   *[Exeunt severally*

ACT V.

SCENE I. *The Louvre.*

The King, Queen-Mother, BRANTÔME, TAVANNES, LA ROCHE-
FOUCAULD, TELIGNY, *and Attendants.*

Charles.

PUT up the dice; you do not play me fair.
    Ca. Indeed the cast did lie too much his way.
La R. Do me right, sir; the chance so thrown on me
May come to serve your hand.
Ch.   Nay, God forbid !
I would not fare so well, lest men should scent
The sudden savor of sharp-relished ills
To snuff my luck behind.   Put them away.
La R. So I may take my leave, my lord, I will.
Ch. Abide a little.
La R.   Sir, in pure faith, I may not.
Ch. Lay down your chariness; I pray you stay;
I am your friend that do entreat you stay
To help me use my better humors well.
La R. This grace of yours doth jar with time in me.
Ca. Fair son, put no dispute in marriage; think,
Our noble friend is yet i' the green of time,
The summer point of wedlock; cross him not.
Ch. No, he shall stay.
Ca.   I love him none the less

That would enfranchise his obedience,
Saying "let pass."

Bra.   I have known an honest lady ·
That would have bit her lips atwain for spite
Sooner than slip her lord's obedience so
And slacken the remitted service of him
For such light points ; I do remember me —

Ca. This tale will hold you, sir.

Bra.   I bade her choose a friend,
She seeming bare of any courtesy
That is well done to such ; I bade her choose —

La R. I take a second leave.

Bra.   As 't were for form, —
" Seeing, look you," said I, " a lady's office is
To endure love and wear a good man's name
As the lace about her wrist " —

Ca.   You shall not go.

La R. Sir, needs I must ; you shall well pardon it.

Bra. She with a face, as thus, let sideways down,
Catching her page i' the eye, — a thing so bearded
As are a woman's lips —

Ca.   My lord Bourdeilles,
I pray you take my way, I 'll hear this out.

Bra. Please you so suffer me —

Ca.   Fair son, good night.

         [*Exeunt* CATH., BRANT., *and Attendants.*

Ch. Good night, sweet mother. — Is she truly gone ?
Then I will pray you leave not me to-night ;

I 'll not to bed ; I would not have you go ;
Yea, by God's blood, I put my heart indeed
Into this prayer of mine.   Come, pleasure me ;
It might avail you ; what, by God's own face,
I think I sue to you.   Is this much alms
That you should please me ?

 La R.   Sir, for my poor half,
I must tie thanks upon the neck of No
And turn him forth of me.

 · *Ch.*   Then you keep here ?

 La R. Good faith, I cannot so ; and I well think
This lord speaks with me.

 Tel.   Even your sense, indeed.

 Ch. You use me hardly, but my wish to you
Lives none the less a good and honest wish ;
So, if my meaning tastes not sweet to you,
Farewell, yea well.   One see my dear friends out.

 La R., Tel. Good night, fair lord.

       [*Exeunt* LA ROCH. *and* TEL.

 Ch.   I would have kept them yet.
So, if a man have sight of a big stone,
And will needs trip and sprawl with a bruised head,
Is it my fault that show him such a stone ?
Or say one filches a fair sword of mine
To rip himself at side, is my sin there ?
Nay not'that much, but walking with my sword
It galls him in the thigh ; am I his hurt?
Twice, yea now thrice, if you shall mark me, sir,

Yea, God knows well I sued three times to them,
I would have had all scars keep off their flesh,
But God's will is not so.

Tav.   You do the wiser
To let them pass.

Ch.   Why truly so I think.
But I am heart-stung for these; this Téligny
That might have laid a word of help my way
And kept such sullen lips of doubtfulness,
I have loved him well. The other, see you, sir,
I have twined arms with him, fed from his eyes,
Made a large pleasure out of usual things
Wherein his lot fell evenly with mine,
Laid my heart on him; yea, this singled man
Was as the kin made closest to my flesh
And in the dearest of my secret will
Did as a brother govern. But he may go;
I were fallen wrong too far to pity him;
So, though they mainly mar him with their pikes,
Stab till the flesh hath holes like a big net,
I will not think I am compassionate;
Yea, though my thought of him pricks me at brain,
I will believe I do not pity him.
Show me the matter of your place, your way,
The measure of your men; nay, my sweet lord,
Pray you hold fast on this; be not made pitiful.
Nay, but stand sure; nay, I beseech you, sure.

                             [*Exeunt*

SCENE II. *Denise's Apartment.*

Enter DENISE.

Den. It is the time ; had but this solid eaith
A capable sense of peril, it should melt
And all disjoint itself ; the builded shape of things
Should turn to waste and air.   It is as strange
As is this perilous intent, that men
Should live so evenly to-night ; talk, move,
Use contemplation of all common times,
Speak foolishly, make no more haste to sleep
Than other days they do ; I have not seen
A man to-day seem graver in the mouth,
Wear slowness on his feet, look sideways out,
Make new the stuff and subject of his speech,
Reason of things, matter of argument,
For such a business.   I see death is not feared,
Only the circumstance and clothes of death ;
Or else men do not commune more with time
Nor have its purpose in them larger writ
Than a beast has.   Why, I did surely think
Such ill foreknowledge would have mastered me
Quite beyond reason ; wrenched my sense away,
Brought it to dull default.   But I do live and stir ;
Have reasonable breath within my lips :
Keep my brain sound, and all my settled blood
Runs the right way.   Perhaps I sleep and dream
That such things are as my fear dotes upon.

Why then I should be mad ; and being mad
I might hold sound opinion of my wit
When it were truly flawed. If I not dream
And have no passionate mixture in my brain,
Large massacre to-night should fill itself
With slaughtered blood and the live price of men.
Why this ? forsooth because of that and that,
For this man's tongue and that man's beard or gait,
For some rank slip of their opinion.
I see full reason why men slay for hate,
But for opinion or slack accident
I get no cause at all. Then I am mad
That I do think what works so much awry
And is past reason so, the natural sense
Doth sicken in receiving it for news,
To be the absolute act and heart of truth.
I will not credit this. Yet wherefore am I
So used as prisoner here ? why taxed with sin ?
Why watched and kept so hard ? called murderess ?
I 'll be assured of it. You jailer, you —
And yet I am afraid to call her forth.
O, she is come.

Enter YOLANDE.

Yol.   Did you not call for me ?

Den. I think I did cry out, being moved in sleep:
I had a dream of you.

Yol.   Ay, had you so ?
And I had set a waking thought on you.

Den. What time is it?

Yol.   Just hard upon eleven.

Den. I have slept four hours.   I pray you tell me now,

As you are gentle, — I do love you much, —

Is it my dream I am a prisoner?

Yol. Did you not call me jailer?

Den.   True, I did.

Now I begin to patch my dream again

And find the colors right.   I dreamed I was

Some sort of evil beast that loved a man,

And the man's heel did bruise it in the neck.

Yol. Take heed of it; you were a snake by this.

Den. I do not know; it may be such I was.

I dreamed of you too; for you took me up

And hid me in a cage and gave me food, —

I think I was a kind of dismal bird, —

And having eaten of your seed and drunk

Water more sharp than blood, I waxed all through

Into a dull disease of overgrowth

And so was choked to death; and men there came

That roasted me for food, and having eaten

All suddenly did break in twain and die.

That was the dream.

Yol.   It was a foolish one.

Den. Then I fell back to dream of one like you

Who held me prisoner; which was dangerous;

For I, being grown to mad rebellion,

Took thought to kill you.

Yol.   That dream was not so good.

Den. Why do.I say all this ? Let me get hence,

Only the little part in heaven I have

I 'll kill myself; nay, by God's name I will.

Yol. Do your own way.

Den.   You shall be taxed with it,

(As I, more harmless, am) being guard of me ;

I will find ways to leave the tax on you.

Yol. Pleasure yourself ; I bid you not refrain.

Den. It is a most poor mercy that I ask.   .

Yol. Too much for me.

Den.   O, it is less in worth

Than God spares barest men ; the most base need on

     earth

Is richer in his pity than you are

In charitable use of me, who am

Too little for your scorns.

Yol.   I will not do it.

Den. Some prayers, long while denied, are sweeter held

For being late granted ; do not so with mine ;

I will be thankful more than beggars are,

Made rich with grant too soon.

Yol.   Plead not to me ;

I have no patience in my ears for you.

Den. Think how you use me ; even kings do leave

Some liberty to the worst worm alive,

Some piece of mercy ; but you, more hard than kings,

Show no such grace as the great jailers do

That wear at waist the keys of the world. You know
'T is better be whole beggar and have flesh
That is but pinched by weather out of breath,
Than a safe slave with happy blood i' the cheek
And wrists ungalled. There 's nothing in the world
So worth as freedom ; pluck this freedom out,
You leave the rag and residue of man
Like a bird's back displumed. That man that hath not
The freedom of his name, and cannot make
Such use as. time and place would please him with,
But has the clog of service at his heel
Forbidding the sound gait; this is no man
But a man's dog ; the pattern of a slave
Is model for a beast.

    Yol.   What do you mean by this ?

    Den. To show you what unworthy pain it is
Your office lays on me.

    Yol.   It is my place ;
My faith is taken to assure you thus,
And you have bought such usage at my hands
By your own act.

    Den.   No, by your life, I have not.

    Yol. You are impeached and must abide the proof.

    Den. The proof, — ay, proof; do, put me to the proof.
There is not proof enough upon me known
To stop a needle's bore. The man now dead
I held my friend, was sorry for his death,
Not pricked for guilt of it. Poor fool, I would

That I had borrowed such a death of him
And left him better times to boot than do
Keep company with me.

Yol. I would you had.

Were one no better dead than stained so much?
I think so ; for myself, in such a scale
The weights were easy to make choice of.

Den. I would not die.

Yol. Did you not say his share were easier borne ?

Den. 'T is like I said so ; yet I would live long.

Yol. Why would you so ? is there such grace in you
To wear out all the bar and thwart of time
And take smooth place again ? The life you have,
Like a blown candle held across the wind,
Dies in the use of it ; you are not loved,
Or love would kiss out shame from either cheek,
New-join the broken patience in your eyes,
Comfort the pain of your so scarred repute
Where the brand aches on it ; honored you are not,
For the loud breath of many-mouthed esteem
Cries harsher on you than on common thieves
When they filch life and all ; you are not secure,
For the most thin divisions of a day
That score the space between two breaths, to you
Are perilous implements edged with all hate
To use upon your life ; you are not happy either,
For guilty, shame doth bruise your side with lead,
- Or clean, why rumor stabs you in the face,

Spits in your mouth. What sweet is in this life
That you would live upon ?

Den.   I do not know ;
But I would live ; though all things else be sharp,
Death stays more bitter than them all ; I would not
Touch lips with death.

Yol.   No ? I have no such doubt.

Den. Is it your place to make me friends with death ?

Yol. It is my pity.

Den.   I should find it so
Were I the cushion for a fool's feet, or
A fool indeed of yours.

Yol.   I called you none.

Den. I were the bell i' the worst fool's cap alive
If I rang right to this wrong breath of yours.
You talk to get me harmed.

Yol.   Put off that fear.

Den. I will not, truly ; you would talk me out,
Be rid of me this whispering way, this fashion
That pulls on death by the ear ; I feel your wisdom ;
'T is craft thick-spun, but I shall ravel it.

Yol. This is your garment that you thrust me in.

Den. It must not be so late ; there will be time ;
I was a fool to call it over late.
Give up your keys.

Yol.   What madness bites you now ?

Den. She called you jailer ; give me up the keys ;
You have the keys ; the outer door is fast ;

If this be madness I am friends with it;
Give me the keys.

Yol.   Will you put hands on me?

Den. I 'll have them out, though God would make you
man
To use me forcibly.

Yol.   I have none such;
Threaten me not, or you shall smite yourself.

Den. I say, the keys.

Yol.   What will you do to me?

Den. Keep there, you get not out.

Yol.   Are you stark crazed?

Den. It may look like enough. What chain is that?
Give me the chain.

Yol.   I swear I have them not.

Den. I do not ask for them. Give me the chain;
Pray you now, do; good truth you are not wise
To use me so; I know you have no keys.
Give me the chain; soft, soft —

Yol.   Here are the keys.
Take them and let me pass.

Den.   I thank you, no;
If I be mad I must do warily,
Or they will trap me. Get you into my chamber;
Now am I twice the sinew of all you
And twice as wise. I say, get in; God's love!
How you do pull my patience! in sound wits
It were too hard to bear. Make haste, I say.

                  [*Exeunt severally.*

SCENE III.   *A Cabinet.*

Enter the Queen-Mother *and* TAVANNES.

Ca. So, you did see them forth ?

Tav.   Madam, I did ;
The king doth fare by this more temperately.

Ca. If he turn white and stagger at his point,
It is too late.   The mortal means of danger
Are well abroad ; and this sole work o' the world
Fit to set hands to.   How do you feel by this ?

Tav. Why, well ; as if my blood were full of wine.

Ca. I am hot only in the palm of the hands.
Do you not think, sir, some of these dead men,
Being children, dreamed perhaps of this ? had fears
About it ? somewhat plucked them back, who knows,
From wishing to grow men and ripen up
For such a death to thrust a sickle there ?

Tav. I never found this woman mixed in you.

Ca. No. — I am certain also that this hour
Goes great with child-birth and with fortunate seed,
Worth care to harvest ; sons are born and die,
Yea, and choke timeless in the dead strait womb,
Of whom we know not ; each day breeds worse ; it is
The general curse of seasons.

Tav.   Well, what help ?

Ca. True. — It hurts little for a man to die,
If he be righteous.   Were I a swordsman born,
A man with such red office in my hands

As makes a soldier, — it would touch me not
To think what milk mine enemy's mouth had drunk,
When both were yearlings a span long. My God!
It is too foolish that conceit of blood
Should stick so on the face; I must look red;
Give me the little mirror-steel; now see;
Here is no painting.

    Tav.   Yea, but let me go.

    Ca. It is man's blood that burns so deep and bites
No crying cleans it. If one kill a dog,
The spot sticks on your skirt as water might;
The next rain is a worse thing. Humph! I see;
We have some hot and actual breath in us
That blood lets out; we feed not as they do;
So the soul comes and makes all motion new;
One guesses at it.

    Tav.   Will you go mad for this?

    Ca. No. — If one strike me on the mouth or breast,
And I am hurt and bleed to death, — is that
Murder? I would not kill them for their blood;
God's mercy! wherein can their blood serve me?
Let all go through.

    Tav.   ˙Madam, I take my leave;
All shall run out ere we two speak again.

    Ca. Hark! I hear shots; as God shall pity me,
I heard a shot. Who dies of that? yea, now,
Who lies and moans and makes some inches red?

    Tav. Not for an hour yet; the first dial-rim
Makes the first shot.

Ca.   The noise moves in my head,
Most hotly moves; pray you keep clear of me.
God help my woman's body for a fool's!
I must even sit.

Tav.   Be patient with your cause;
Give it all room, then you get heart again;
I know those ways.

Ca.   Too sharp to drink, too sharp,
Sweet Christ of mine; blood is not well to drink,
God put this cup some little off my mouth.
Yea, there it catches in mine eyes like smoke,
The smell of blood, it stings and makes one weep;
So, God be patient till I breathe again.

Tav. Are you fallen foolish? woman, — madam, —
thou!
Take heart to speak at least.

Ca.   I will take heart.
What is there in it that should bar my breath,
Or make me babble stark across the sense
As I did then? can the flesh merely prate
With no mind in it to fall praying, ha?
Give me some wine. Go out and cheer your men;
Bid them be bold; say, work is worth such pains;
Be quick and dangerous as the fire that rides
Too fast for thunder. Tell them the king, the king
Will love each man, cherish him sweetly, say,
And I will hold him as that brother is
Whom one flesh covered with me. — Will it rain?

Tav. No ; the wide ends of the sky are clear with stars ;
It is broad moon-time.

Ca.   I would fain see rain.
Art thou so slow of purpose, thou great God,
The keenest of thy sighted ministers
Can catch no knowledge what we do ? for else
Surely the wind would be as a hard fire,
And the sea's yellow and distempered foam
Displease the happy heaven ; wash corn with sand
To waste and mixture ; mar the trees of growth ;
Choke birds with salt, breach walls with tided brine
And chase with heavy water the horned brood
Past use of limit ; towers and popular streets
Should in the middle green smother and drown,
And havoc die with fulness. — I should be mad,
I talk as one filled through with wine ; thou, God,
Whose thunder is confusion of the hills
And with wrath sown abolishes the fields,
I pray thee if thy hand would ruin us,
Make witness of it even this night that is
The last for many cradles, and the grave
Of many reverend seats ; even at this turn,
This edge of season, this keen joint of time,
Finish and spare not. If no thunder came
When thou wert full of wrath to the fierce brim,
Next year would spit on worship. — I am faint yet ;
See you, I have to chatter these big words
To keep my head straight ; each small nerve it hath

Is like a chord pulled straight to play upon
Till the string ache at sound.   Sir, bear with me.

   Tav. Keep but soft speech. ` Nay, pray you let me go ;
Open the door ; I should be hence in time.

                    [*The* King of Navarre *passes over the stage.*

   Ca. Good night, lord marshal.   You come late, fair sir,
To bear my daughter commendations.
I doubt she looks for you ; I have had pains
To bring her safe and presently your way ;
She had some will to watch.

   Hen.   I am the more bound to you.

   Ca. Let my praise sleep to-night, unless you do
Speak well of me to her.   See, the white stars
Do burn upon the fair blue weather's waste
Thick as the lulled wind carries the marred leaves ;
Yea, see how gray my likenesses are grown,
That grow on my gray years !

   Hen.   Madam, good night.   [*Exit.*

   Ca. That gives one heart ; and yet I seem to choke,
I shall feel weak till I do hear them shoot.
Pray you take order that the watch be sharp
Upon this boy.

   Tav.   I shall take order.

   Ca.   Yea,
But go with me till I have seen the king.   [*Exeunt.*

SCENE IV. *A Street.*

Enter GUISE *with Soldiers.*

Gui. Keep in, let no man slip across of you ;
Hold well together ; what face I miss of mine
Shall not see food to-morrow ; but he that makes
So dull a mixture of his soul with shame
As spares the gold hair or the white, shall be
Dead flesh this hour.   Take iron to your hands,
Fire to your wills ; let not the runagate love
Fool your great office ; be pity as a stone
Spurned either side the way.   That breast of woman
That suckles treason with false milk and breeds
Poison i' the child's own lip, think not your mother's ·
Nor that lank chin which the gray season shakes
Hold competent of reverence.   Pluck me that corn
Which alters in the yellow time of man ;
And the sick blade of ungrown days disroot,
The seed makes rot the flower.   There's no such use
But reason turns to holy, and keen right
Washes as pure as faith ; therefore be swift, and let
Cold mercy choke on alms.

A Captain.   We shall not fail.

Gui. Some ten go with me to the admiral's house ;
You shall be one, — and you ; pluck him from bed,
And use his body as your edges please,
Then hale him through the street.   The rest of you,
As you see time, fire either way ; then draw,

7*

And strike across the thickest ends of flight,
God helping you.   Say "Guise" now and set on.

[*Exeunt.*

SCENE V.   *The Admiral's House.*

Enter COLIGNY *and* LA NOUE.

La N.   That this is true we have clean proofs ; she hath
made us
Pawns of her game ; this very France of ours
Is as a cloth to wipe her feet upon,
Her bed and stool of lust ; and hath put on
The naked patience of a beaten face
And sufferance of a whore.

Co.   I think so.   Sir,
I have believed this marriage of Navarre
Began our waste.

La N.   That stings me not so hard
As that men mix us in their mouths with fools
Who are not worth our slight esteem of them,
And yet have sewn religion on their sleeve
And badged their caps with us.

Co.   They have done more harm ;
There is no lean or lesser villany
That war or peace-time saddles them withal.
But it must be our blame, the fault of it
Throws dirt on us and each man's several hand
That wets no finger in the Catholic way ;
That bites the nearest.

La N.   We are imperilled ; well,
Danger should be the coat across my back,
Meat in my lips, if I saw clear and good
The choice and shape of our necessity ;
But here to blunder the chance out, — my lord,
No help for us then here ?
     Co.   I see no help.
Nay too, I bind not all the weight on them ;
In me and you the plague is well at work
That rots all chances.   We have let go the times
That came with gold in the hands ; and that slow snake,
Impotent patience of pernicious things,
Hath won upon us, and blown murderous breath
Between the wide unwardered lips of sleep.
Come, talk no more.   Is the night fair ? methinks
I heard some humming rumors run through it.
     La N. Sir, fair enough ; there goes a little wind
Among the roofs, but slow as a maimed man ;
The skies burn sharp with point of the lit stars,
Even to the larger cope of all there is
No air but smooth.
     Co.   'T is a good night for sleep ;
Fair time to you.
     La N.   I pray God set such peace
Upon the seasonable eyes of sleep
As may well comfort you.   Dear lord, good night. [*Exit.*
     Co. Farewell. — Now might I put lean patience in my
          prayers

If I should pray to-night ; I have no will
To leave my witness against men and pray
That God would suffer them.   Surely I think he bears
Somewhat too much with such side-working sins
As lame the laboring hope of men, and make
Endurance a blind sort of sleepy lie
To confute God with.   This woman here grows old,
As I am old ; we have drawn this way and that
So long, the purpose lessens from the doing,
Turns to a very function of the flesh
So used for custom.   She carries France her way,
And my way breaks.   Then if one sees the end,
The goal that shuts the roadway sheer across,
The builded limit of a complete will,
All these side-briers and puddled rain-shallows
That rend or drench us, are but naught thereto.
Well, here I tire for one, and fain would use
This winter of bleached hair and fallen flesh
To make me quiet room. — Shut up the house ;
Let nothing wake the windows. — I will to bed. —
The wind gets thick indeed.   What noise is there ?

[Firing on side.

Get me a light.

   Gui. (*Within.*) Nay, but get you first in ;
Throw the knave out at window.

   Co.   Yea, my Guise ?
Then are the sickles in this corn, I doubt.

   Gui. (*Within.*) This way, men, this !

   Co.   ·   Not so ; the right hand, sirs.

SCENE VI. *Outside the Louvre.*

Enter DENISE.

Den. I cannot find a man ; the cries are thick ;
I come too late. Alas, I fear the king
Hath put the order forward ; I may see him
And so prevent some peril ; and though they slay me,
I die of my misdoing. Yet I fear death
Most piteously, wear passion on my cheek.
White as a coward's. I 'll yet forth and look ;
For in the temper of this bloody time
Must sleep my help or end ; I may discover him
And that may be some grace ; now God be good,
Or I am so far bruised this way, as death
Can bite no sharper.   [*Exit.*

SCENE VII. *A Balcony of the Louvre.*

Enter many Ladies.

1 *La.* Did you not see him ?

2 *La.*   Give me place, place, place ;
I have the news.

3 *La.*   Not you ; I can say more.

2 *La.* How your sides push ! let me get breath — O
      Mary !
I have seen such things —

4 *La.*   As should wear silence.

2 *La.*   Nay,
For they felt sweet.

3 *La.*   See, there goes one, — and there ;
O well run, you ! now trip him, — 'ware stones, ho !
Or you may catch a bruise.

1 *La.*   Now is he down.

5 *La.* Not so ; you have no eyes.

3 *La.*   Had I a bow,
I would take four myself.   Look, look, a chase !
O, now you thrust.

4 *La.*   Way, sirs ! make way for him !

5 *La.* There 's a child slain ; I will not look that side ;
They thrust him in the back.

2 *La.*   Go and sew threads ;
Go sew ; you are a fool.

1 *La.*   Who has that side ?

4 *La.* Do him no hurt, sirs ; yea, the point now, yea,
Not the edge, — look you ! just the nape across, —
Down with him, there !

3 *La.*   Is the old man yet slain ?

2 *La.* Ay, by the Guise ; they took him in his bed,
Just in a fumbled sheet.

· 1 *La.*   No, he was risen.

Enter RENÉE.

Renée. Why are you here ? next room serves best for
    show ;
There they have drawn to head, that all the street
Swells up and cries ; Soubise and Marsillac
Hold off their pikes.

4 *La.*   Show us the way to that.

Renée. This way,— I pray you hurt me not, —this way;
Do not push close. God's love, what heat is here!

                                                    [*Exeunt.*

SCENE VIII. *The Streets.*

Enter GUISE, TAVANNES, *with* Soldiers; MARSILLAC, SOU-
BISE, PARDAILLAN, *and others confusedly.*

Sol. Guise, Guise! down with them! for the king, the
    king!
Guise, Guise!   .

1 *Sol.*   Here, dog, take this to choke upon.

Mar. Sirs, stand by me; hew down that knave at right,
I pray you, sir. Nay, we shall spoil them yet;
Stand but a little fast.

A Huguenot. -   Mercy! God help!

Tav. Thrust me a steel nail in that tongue and throat;
So, sir; prate now as you do love such nails.
Set on; this August serves for reaping-time;
Bleed the plague out with your incisions.

Mar. Guise, if thou hast a man's mark left on thee,
Do me this right. I thank you, sir; the office
Spares me some work.

Gui.   Stand to me, men; down with him!
My heel hath rent a better face to-night.

Tav. Kill me this scapegate harlot in her smock,
The child to water. Charge their face again;
Make a clean way and we shall smite them all.

Par. Yea, devil's dog, wilt only snarl at me?
Prithee, but room to die in and take breath,
One stifles this way stupidly,—ah, beasts!   [*Dies.*

> *Tav.* (*Crossing Soubise.*) Ah thing, what set thee on such
> work to do?

Die, fragment, and turn carrion fit for use.   [*Stabs him.*
There 's not a man the less.

Sol.   Tavannes! Tavannes!

Others. Guise, Guise! upon them for the king, the king!

                                        [*Exeunt.*

SCENE IX.   *The Louvre.*

The Queen-Mother, YOLANDE, MARGARET, Duchess of Lorraine, *and Attendants.*

Ca. Where is the king?

Yol.   Madam, gone forth I think.

Ca. Are you whole yet? you look half slain with fear;
Quiet yourself.

Mar.   You know not what I saw.
No, not your hand; let me sit here.

Ca.   Yea, sit.—
O, are you there?

Yol.   Madam, it is no fault
To say she is escaped.

Ca.   No fault!
What, have you let her go? how came she out?

Yol. Do your best will with me; I will speak truth.

Ca. How came she forth? you are a worthy guard,—

Do, as you love the better chance of time.
I have a will to smite you by the cheek;
Answer to that.

Yol.   By heaven I speak all pure;
By heaven I do; she had the key of me.,

Ca. Do not you mock; I may turn sharp with you.

Yol. Alas, I do not ; she put force on me
To let her forth ; I could not please you ; do not
Lay your great wrath my way.

Ca.   O fool, — fool, — fool!
Were you so much compassionate of her ?
I was bewitched to give you such a charge.
Where is she now ? speak still.

Yol.   I have not seen.

Ca. If these be lies I 'll find a bitter way, —
I 'll do, — I have no time to think of it,
But I 'll make shame as wide as your desert
To show your penitence. Find me this girl,
Or punishment shall reach beyond your deed,
Put pity out of service. Look for her ;
Bring her to me ; if I so miss her, — Go. [*Exit* YOLANDE.
How does my daughter ?

Duch.   Madam, well by this.

Mar. But shaken to the brain.

Ca.   Poor child ; what cause ?

Mar. I was unclothed for sleep, heavy at eyes,
And fit for my bed's heat, when thus at point
There comes a cry and beating of two hands

K

Hard at my door ; then snaps the hinge from it,
And a man comes, smeared shamefully and red
With a new wound i' the side ; flings him on me,
Plucks me half slain with fear across the bed,
Cries for some pity, hales me by the hand,
And so clings hard ; when my great fear got strength
To wellnigh wrench me clear and throw off him,
Begins such piteous prayer and puts rebuke
To such a tune, so bitter, I did even
Make mercy wet with tears ; whereon (as peril
Would outgrow its own face and turn like death,
Doubling my fear) the soldiers after him,
Some three or four, flecked murderously with blood,
All weaponed for their work, and crying out,
Broke in on us ; he twisting with sore fright
Obscures himself with me ; and thus in doubt
He shuffled this side death ; for as they bore on him
Still holding to me, comes their captain in,
Chides the knave off that had a hand on us,
And plucks him loose ; then with mixt laughter did
Swear the man safe ; he could not choose but laugh
To see me harried so, so haled and drawn,
Nor 'I to see him laugh ; and so our laughter
Got off my friend.

Enter the King *with an arquebuse, and* TAVANNES.

Ch.   O, are you here ? I have
Some three — some six — by God I have some six
Already to my share.

Ca. (*To Tav.*)   Sir, what is this ?

Tav. The king has slain some six of them, he says ;
I saw him shoot indeed.

Ch.   Ay, did I not ?
Hear you, he says I did ; hear him a little.
One — two — see, I can take them either hand,
The place is wide.

Tav.   Here, by this balcony ;
I saw him shoot myself.

Ca.   How goes the work ?

Tav. Even like a wave that turns ; the thing opposed
Is as the weed it rends at root away,
Dies ere the touch for fear.

Ca.   It is well done.

Tav. The king did summon me to speak with ; there
I left them midways.   Are you yet abashed ?
I think it smirches you with half a red,
This pity ; are you nothing plagued with it ?

Ca. Not I a jot ; I would all such i' the world
Were here to be so rid.

Re-enter YOLANDE.

                  Now ? have you her ?

Yol. She has been seen to-night ; one found her late
Ranging the rooms and passage of the court
Like one distempered ; now catching at this man
To pray him pity her, crying on him
To let her go ; or poring in side ways

To follow up their feet, as she would trace
The consequence and graft of peril through
To know it thoroughly.

Ca.   This doth approve it like
That she is fled; where should she hide herself?

Yol. Madam, the main half of your ladies are
Gone forth to gaze upon this slaughter.

Ca.   Ay!
May she be there? Lord marshal, have you seen
These ladies that she talks of?

Tav.   Madam, I have;
They were about the windows next the street
Searching each side with large and curious eyes;
I saw some twenty with sweet laughing mouths
And hair wherein the flame of lights did make
New colors red as blood, gathered upon
A corpse I slew myself, with fleers and gibes
Abusing the blind thing; it made me merry
To hear how they did mock the make of it,
As blood were grown their game.

Ca.   The king is sad;
I have a word like mercy in my mind,
But it doth wound itself; I see no use
That sorrow fails not in, where things are done
That will not be wept out.

Tav.   'T is a strange night;
But not to me displeasing; I esteem
Our service wholesome. I will not forth again,
For I have watched into a weariness.

Ca. How does our son ?

Ch.   I think some runagates be
Yet by this passage. Give me that again ;
I 'll score them too. Nay, if one wet his knees,
Best over ears and all.   [*Exit.*

Ca.   They are too far to hit;
I 'll wager them safe out. What do you see ?

Tav. They have escaped the points o' the guard ; I
     doubt
He will not bear it so.

Yol.   O, that way — there —
Can you make out? a woman as I think —

Ca. Some poor man's wife ; I would she might get safe.

Tav. See, the king thrusts out far ; 't is a brave king ;
Look how his bowing body crooks itself
After the aim.

Ca.   Ten pieces to a doit
The issue scars not her.

Tav.   I take you, madam.
The king comes back.

Re-enter King.

Ca.   Have I waged wrong on you?

Ch. I have slain seven. Mother, I could begin
To sicken of this way.

Ca.   What way, fair son ?

Ch. I did not think the blood should run so far.
There was a woman I saw lately slain,

And she was ript i' the side ; at point to die,
She threw her on her child and there came one
Who clove it by the throat.   Then I grew sick
And my head seemed to change as if the stroke
Had dulled it through the bone ; the sense of that
Still aches in me.
  Ca.   Set your thought otherwise.
  Ch. Why so I do ; and cannot choose but think
How many that rose fresh with wholesome thoughts
And with my credit washed their faiths in me
Do sleep now bloodily.
  Ca.   You hurt yourself
To lay repentance on such deeds as are
Necessity's mere proof.   Put this away ;
And tell yourself how many dead in war
Gave battle welcome and their time went out
Even in the wording of it ; and but for this
(Though I confess the sense feels sick on it)
We should have had worse wars.
  Ch.   I think we might.
  Ca. Bethink you too, what stings us in the seeing,
It is no new infection of the world
Corrupting all its usual office, or
The common blood of it, with some strange sore,
More gross being new ; such things have chanced ere this,
Yea, many thousand times have men put hand
To a worse business, and given hire to death
To captain them i' the field and play their man,

Used him with fellowship. Who knows, sweet son,
But here, and in this very Paris, where
Our work now smells abhorred, some such may come
To try more bloody issues, and break faith
More shamefully? make truth deny its face,
Kill honor with his lips, stab shame to death,
Unseat men's thoughts, envenom all belief,
Yea, spit into the face and eyes of God
His forsworn promise? Such things may be ; for time,
That is the patient ground of all men's seed
And ripens either corn alike, may bring
Deeds forth which shall as far outreach our act
As this doth common things; and so they wear
The clothes and cover of prosperity,
Those tongues where blame of us yet sticks shall put
Applause on them.
  Ch.   It may be you say true ;
I would believe you with a perfect will.

   Enter RENÉE, ANNE, *and others, with* DENISE.

 Ca. What is this business? quick —
 Ch.   O now, now, now —
This is the very matter of my thought
That was a ghost before ; this is the flesh,
The bone and blood of that my thin surmise,
Palpably shaping fear. I will not see her.
 Ca. How fell this out ? you, speak.
 Renée.   We found her so —
Wounded I think to death.

Anne.   She hath besought us
To bring her to this presence.

Ca.   Can she speak still?

Anne. Yea, and speak straight; I would not pawn my
     word
This touch were deadly to her.

Renée.   I say it is;
She has a wound i' the side.

Ca.   Set her down gently;
She will do well; deal softly with her; good;
Be heedful of your hands. So; look to her.

Den. I thank you, madam; let me sit a little.

Mar. Give her some wine.

Den.   Sir, are not you the king?
He was grown kind; let them not slay me then,
I 'll swear you are no less. I think I am hurt;
Let me speak to you; my side hurts indeed.

Ch. Nay, if hell come in sleep, then hell itself
Is like the face of a dream. Eh? this were quaint,
To find such hell at last.

Den.   I thank you too;
For I am well, so near the heart of quiet,
The most hushed inward of obscuréd peace,
I feel my spirit a light thing and sweet,
Evened with what it was.

Ca.   Hath she a hurt indeed?

Yol. Yea, the right side; she holds her gown on it.

Ca. I did believe this was the stab of fear.

Get her away. — My son, remove your arms.
Some one fetch help; but not too quickly, mark,

[*Aside to* YOLANDE, *who goes out.*

Lest speed undo itself. — Release her, sir.
Den. No, let him hold me safe ; your hand that side,
I shall breathe better. Do they still slay ? Alas,
It is a night shall mark you red forever
I' the honest eyes of men.
    Ca.   Will she talk now?
    Ch. How came this hurt on you ?
    Ca.   Make that no question.
    Ch. Will you teach me ? Here, sweet, this way; you know
I always loved you. — Give us room ; she will
Get present breath.
    Den.   It was a window-shot, —
A side-shot striking by the wall; O God !
It pains me sore ; but ease me with your arm.
    Ch. Is God fallen old at once, that he is blind
And slays me not ? I am beneath all hell,
Even past the limit and conceit of reach
Where fire might catch on me. Why, I have slain
The chiefest pearl o' the world, the perfect rule
To measure all sweet things ; now even to unseat God
Were a slight work.
    Den.   Was it your aim indeed ?
    Ch. O no, no aim. Get me some help ; all you
That gape and shiver on this act enstaged,
You are all parts of murder.

8

Ca.   Sir, be patient ;
This cross is not your sin. — He heeds us not ;
Do not speak to him.

Ch.   Is she yet warm ?   I 'll give
That man that will but put an hour in her
My better part of kingdom.   Nay, look up ;
This breath that I do speak to thee withal
Shall be the medicine to restore thine own
Though I spend all.   Sweet, answer me ; I 'll make thee
Queen of my present power and all that earth
Which hangs upon it.

Den.   Disquiet not yourself;
I do not chide you ; nay, I know too, sir,
You never hated me ; nor did I ever
Make such a fault as should have plucked me thus
Into your hate or stroke.   I am dead indeed ;
And in this flesh hath God so scourged your act
As I now bleed for it ; so I do think
That from this time his adverse hand will not
Push your loss further.

Mar.   This is a bitter sight.

Ca. A pitiful ; but come you not into 't ;
You have no part.

Den.   I tax you not for it.
I have good hope that you have done herein
Mere blind man's work, not put upon your hands
Murder's own wear ; which ministry of yours
God punishes in me.   Too much of that.

Do not you yet for this my foolish sake
Make dull your better seasons ; let remorse,
If such will bite, feed otherwise than here ;
For me, indeed I leave no blur of it
To blot your love at all. For my grace given
Give me grace back ; change mercy with me, for
I have wronged you too. In this large world, dear lord,
I have so little space I need use time
With most scant thrift ; yet that my love holds out
Let me catch breath to say. No, stir not yet ;
Be but two minutes patient of me ; keep
Your arm more straight. Say I have slain myself
And the thought clears you ; be not moved thereat ;
For though I slew a something that you loved
I did it lovingly.   [*Dies.*

   Ca.   Ay, there it breaks ;
I am sorry for her, she was fair enough.
Doth she not breathe ?

   Ch.   No whit ; the lips are dull.
Now could I rail God out of pity, change
The blessed heaven with words ; yea, move sphered
    souls
Into a care of me ; but I 'll say nothing ;
No reason stands I should say anything, -
Who have this red upon my soul. Yea, dead ?
She is all white to the dead hair, who was
So full of gracious rose the air took color,
Turned to a kiss against her face. Sirs, help ;

I would fain have her hence; I am bound to you;
Sirs, hurt her not to touch her side; yea, so.

                  [Exit, with some bearing out the body.

    Ca. (*To Tav.*) Come hither, sir; as you respect my grace,
Lay your good care on him, that in waste words
His mood gall not himself.   For this girl slain,
Her funeral privacy of rite shall be
Our personal care; though her deserts were such
As crave no large observance, yet our pity
Shall almost cover the default in them
With all smooth grace that grace may do to her.
You to my son, and you this way with me;
The weight of this harsh dawn doth bruise my sense,
That I am sick for sleep.   Have care of him.

ROSAMOND.

ROSAMOND.

———•———

I. *The Maze at Woodstock.*

ROSAMOND, CONSTANCE.

Constance.

TAKE not such thought of it.
   Ros.   Nay, I take none;
They cannot put me out of love so much
As to take thought for them; yet I am hurt
And my sense wrung at this a little. See,
If six leaves make a rose, I stay red yet
And the wind nothing ruins me; who says
I am at waste? — Look, since last night! — for me,
I care not though you get through all they said.
All this side dashed with fits of weeping time,
See you, the red struck out; an evil year.
If such times vex me till no sleep feels good,
It is not that I think of such lewd words
With wine still hot in them. Who calls it spring?
Simply this winter plays at red and green.
Clean white no color for me, did they say?

I never loved white roses much; but see
How the wind drenches the low lime-branches
With shaken silver in the rainiest leaves.
Mere winter, winter. I will love you well,
Sweet Constance, do but say I am not fair;
No need for patience if I be not fair,
For if men really lie to call me fair
He need not come; I pray God keep him close
For fear he come and see I am not fair.
Can you not speak, not say if this be true,
That I may cease? come, am I fair or no?
Speak your pure mind.

    Const.   Nay, madam, for you know
Doubtless it was delight to make your face
And rippled soft miraculous gold hair
Over the touched veins of most tender brows
Meant for men's lips to make them glad of God
Who gives them such to kiss.

    Ros.   Leave off my praise,   ·
It frets me flesh and all as sickness doth
Till the blood wanes; yea, and quaint news to hear,
That I am fair, have hair strung through with gold,
Smooth feet, smooth hands, and eyes worth pain to see!
Why once the king spake of my hair like this,
"As though rain filled and stained a tress of corn
Loose i' the last sheaf of many slackened sheaves;
Or if" (ay, thus) "one blew the yellow dust
That speckles a red lily off both cheeks

Held in the sun, so if in kissing her
I let the wind into her hair, it blows
Thin gold back, shows the redder thread of it,
Burnt saffron-scented "; some faint rhyme of his
Tuned round and colored after his French wise.

    Const. You learnt such sonnets of him? — A man's
      step, —
Ah, that girl's binding the wet tendrils there
Last night blew over.

    Ros.   See, at my hand's end,
Those apple-flowers beaten on a heap,
So has the heavy weather trod on them.
There are my rhymes all spoilt and blown with wind,
Broken like birds' wings blown against a wall.
Girl, do you know I lived so quiet once,
Leaning whole days in a warmed side-window
With the chin cushioned up and soft vague feet
Thrust out to sleep, and warm sides couched for ease
Full of soft blood, pulsed slow with happiness
Such fair green seasons through, with dreams that lay
Most blossom-soft between the lids, — and love
A little way I thought above my brows,
His finger touching them; yea, for whole months
I was so patient to serve time and have
Love's mouth at last set suddenly on mine;
Abode and heard the blood that grew in me
More sweet, and the days' motion in my ears
Touched audibly.

    8*   L

Const.   This was a gracious time.

Ros. One song you have, I pray but sing me that,
I taught it you; and yet I like it not;
Trouveres have sweet lips with a bitter heart,
And such a gracious liar, I doubt, wrote this;
But sing it; it shall do no harm to hear.

    Const. Sweet, for God's love I bid you kiss right close
        On mouth and cheek, because you see my rose
          Has died that got no kisses of the rain;
        So will I sing to sweeten my sweet mouth,
        So will I braid my thickest hair to smooth,
          And then, — I need not call you love again.
I like it well enough.

    Ros.   The sick sweet in it
Taints my mouth through. — Could the heat make me
    sleep!
My feet ache like my head. — Doth this I say
Tire you so hard you cannot answer me?

    Const. Madam, I would my words were wine to drink
That might heal all your better sense and blood;
But some hurts ache in the bone past oil and wine,
And I do think the words I heard of you
Burn you thus hot only with hate of shame.

    Ros. Shame? who said shame? am I so sick of love.
That shame can hurt me? there's no shame in the world
Whose wound would hurt more than too hard a kiss
If love kept by the face of blinking shame
To kill the pain with patience. Am I his wife

That it should fret me to be trod by shame?
Ah, child, I know that were my lord at right
And shame stood on this left with eager mouth
For some prepared scorn, — I could but turn
Saying, — lo, here this hand to cover me,
Lo, this to plait my hair and warm my lips;
I could well pity thee, dull snake, poor fool,
Faint shame, too feeble to discredit me.
    Const. I would I had never come hither.
    Ros.   Are you tired?
But I seem shameful to you, shameworthy,
Contemnable of good women, being so bad,
So bad as I am. Yea, would God, would God,
I had kept my face from this contempt of yours.
Insolent custom would not anger me
So as you do; more clean are you than I,
Sweeter for gathering of the grace of God
To perfume some accomplished work in heaven?
I do not use to scorn, stay pure of hate, .
Seeing how myself am scorned unworthily;
But anger here so takes me in the throat
I would speak now for fear it strangle me.
Here, let me feel your hair and hands and face;
I see not flesh is holier than flesh,
Or blood than blood more choicely qualified
That scorn should live between them. Better am I
Than many women; you are not over fair,
Nor delicate with some exceeding good

In the sweet flesh ; you have no much tenderer soul
Than love is moulded out of for God's use
Who wrought our double need; you are not so choice
That in the golden kingdom of your eyes
All coins should melt for service. But I that am
Part of the perfect witness for the world
How good it is ; I chosen in God's eyes
To fill the lean account of under men,
The lank and hunger-bitten ugliness
Of half his people; I who make fair heads
Bow, saying, " Though we be in no wise fair
We have touched all beauty with our eyes, we have
Some relish in the hand, and in the lips
Some breath of it," because they saw me once ;
I whose curled hair was as a strong staked net
To take the hunters and the hunt, and bind
Faces and feet and hands ; a golden gin
Wherein the tawny-lidded lions fell,
Broken at ankle ; I that am yet, ah yet,
And shall be till the worm hath share in me,
Fairer than love or the clean truth of God,
More sweet than sober customs of kind use
That shackle pain and stablish temperance ;
I that have roses in my name, and make
All flowers glad to set their color by ;
I that have held a land between twin lips
And turned large England to a little kiss ;
God thinks not of me as contemptible,

And that you think me even a smaller thing
Than your own goodness and slight name of good,
Your special, thin, particular repute ;
I would some mean could be but clear to me
Not to contemn you.

Const.　　　　　Madam, I pray you think
I had no will to whet you to such edge ;
I might wish merely to be clear of pain
Such as I have to see you weep, — to see
That wasp contempt feed on your colored rind
Whose kernel is so spiced with change of sweet ;
No more, I swear to you by God no more.

Ros. I will believe you. But speak truly now
As you are fair, I say you are fair too,
Would you be wiser than I was with him ?
A king to kiss the maiden from your lips,
Fill you with fire as water fills the sea,
Hands in your hair and eyes against your face, —
Ay, more than this, this need not strike at heart,
But say that love had bound you like a dog,
Leashed your loose thoughts to his uncertain feet,
Then would you be much better than such are
As leave their soul upon two alien lips
Like a chance word of talk they use for breath ?
O girl, that hast no bitter touch of love,
No more assurance of it than report
Flaunts in the teeth of blame, — I bid you know
Love is much wiser than we twain, more strong

Than men who hold the pard by throat and jaw.
Love's signet-brand stamps through the gold o' the years,
Severs the gross and chastens out the mould.
.God has no plague so perilous as love,
And no such honey for the lips of Christ
To purge them çlean of gall and sweet for heaven.
It was to fit the naked limbs of love
He wrought and clothed the world with ordinance.
Yea, let no wiser woman hear me say
I think that whoso shall unclothe his soul
Of all soft raiment colored custom weaves,
And choose before the cushion-work of looms
Stones rough at edge to stab the tender side,
Put honor off and patience and respect
And veils and relics of remote esteem
To turn quite bare into large arms of love,
God loves him better than those bitter fools
Whom ignorance makes clean, and bloodless use
Keeps colder than their dreams.

Const.   It may be true,
I know not ; only to stay maiden-souled
Seems worthier to me.

Ros.   Doth it so ?   Ah you
That tie the spirit closer to the flesh
To keep both sweet, it seems again to me
You kill the gracious secret of it, and mar
The wholesome heaven with scent of ruined things
That breed mere flies for issue.   Ay, and love

That makes the daily flesh an altar-cup
To carry tears and rarest blood within
And touch pained lips with feast of sacrament, —
So sweet it is, God made it sweet! Poor words,
Dull words, I have compassion on them, girl,
Their babble falls so far this side of love
Significance faints in them. This I know,
When first I had his arms across my head
And had his mouth upon my heated hair
And his sharp kisses mixed into my blood,
I hung athirst between his hands, and said,
Sweet, and so sweet! for both mine eyes were weak,
Possessed with rigorous prophecy of tears
To drench the lids past sleeping, and both lips
Stark as twain rims of a sweet cup drunk out.

   Const. My first word serves me here ; this may be true.

   Ros. Say this, you have a tender woman's face,
Do you love children ? does it touch your blood
To see God's word finished in a child's face
For us to touch and handle ? seems it sweet
To have such things in the world to hold and kiss ?

   Const. Yea, surely.

   Ros.   Yea? then be most sure of this,
Love doth so well surpass and foil the sense
That makes us pleasure out of children seen,
That I being severed from the lips of mine
Feel never insufficient sight, or loss
Of the sweet natural aim or use in eyes

Because they are not; but for only this ;
That seldom in grave passages of time
Such gracious red possesses the full day
As leaves me light to look into his face
Who made me children.

  Const.   Doth he love you as well ?
Then two such loves were never wrought in flesh
Since the sun moved.

  Ros.   Ah girl, you fail fair truth ;
He doth love me, would let me take his name
To soil, his face to set my feet upon ;
But love is no such new device we need
Boast over that. Nay, are you dull indeed ?
All stories are so lined and sewn with love,
Ravel that gold and broidered thread in them,
You rend across the mid and very seam.
Yea, I am found the woman in all tales,
The face caught always in the story's face ;
I Helen, holding Paris by the lips,
Smote Hector through the head ; I Cressida
So kissed men's mouths that they went sick or mad,
Stung right at brain with me ; I Guenevere
Made my queen's eyes so precious and my hair
Delicate with such gold in its soft ways
And my mouth honeyed so for Launcelot,
Out of good things he chose his golden soul
To be the pearlwork of my treasuring hands,
And so our love foiled God ; I that was these

And am no sweeter now than Rosamond
With most full heart and mirth give my lord up
Body's due breath and soul's forefashioned peace
To pay love with; what should I do but this
That am so loved? Ay, you might catch me here
Saying his French wife smites my love across
With soft strange lips; yea, I know too she may
Pluck skirts of afterthought, kiss pity's feet,
Marry remembrance with a broken ring;
No time so famished, no such idle place
As spares her room next his; a wife, his wife, —
If I be no king's wife, prithee what need
That she should steal the word to dress her name
That suits my name as well? take love, take all;
What shall keep hunger from the word of wife?
What praise, if reputation wear thin shoes,
Shall keep the rain from honored women's feet?
Wife, wife, — I get no music out of wife;
I see no reason between me and wife
But what breath mars with making; yea, poor fool,
She gets the harsh bran of my corn to eat.

Const. Men call the queen an adder underfoot,
Dangerous obedience in the trodden head;
I pray you heed your feet in walking here.

Ros. Fear is a cushion for the feet of love,
Painted with colors for his ease-taking;
Sweet red, and white with wasted blood, and blue
Most flower-like, and the summer-spoused green

And sea-betrothed soft purple and burnt black.
All colored forms of fear, omen and change,
Sick prophecy and rumors lame at heel,
Anticipations and astrologies,
Perilous inscription and recorded note,
All these are covered in the skirt of love
And when he shakes it these are tumbled forth,
Beaten and blown i' the dusty face of the air.
Were she ten queens and every queen his wife,
I could not find out fear.   Where shame is hid
I can but guess when patience leaves me sick ;
But where the lank bat fear is huddled in
Doth no conjecture smell.

 Const.   Mine holds yet out,
Seeing the queen is reconciled : their son
Ties peace between both hands ; she will do much
To move him from his care set over you.

 Ros. I care not ; let her bind him heel to head,
So she may keep him, clip and kiss him so.
For me, I will go in ; no doubt he shall '
Be here to-night ; I were best sleep till then
And have the sweet of sleep about my face
To touch his senses with ; for he shall come,
I have no doubt of him but he shall come.
Kiss me yet, sweet, I would not anger you. [*Exit.*

 Const. Yea, I taste through this way of yours ; so fair
Her sin may serve as well as holy ways,
Shall not it so ?   Let the queen make some tale,

A silk clue taken in the king's spur's gold,
No fear lest I be taken ; and what harm
To catch her feet i' the dragnets of her sin
That is so full of words, eats wicked bread,
Shares portion with shame's large and common cups,
Feeds at lewd tables, girds loose garments on ?
For all this brave breath wasted out of heart,
I doubt this frets her ; verily I think
Some such pain only makes her gibe at me —
Fair fool, with her soft shameful mouth ! at least
I keep clean hands to do God's offices
And serve him with my noose upon her neck.   [*Exit.*

II.   *The Palace at Shene.*

QUEEN ELEANOR *and* ROBERT DE BOUCHARD.

Queen Eleanor.

YEA, true for such ; but he and I were old
   Already, though men say his hair keeps black,
Ay, black-bright hair, touched deep as poppies' black
They cover up in scarlet ; that 's my lord ;
Sweet color, with a thought of black at heart.
Some flowers, they say, if one pluck deep enough,
Bleed as you gather.
   Bouch.   That means love, I think ;
You gather it and there 's the blood at root.

Qu. El. How much, my Bouchard? let your beard alone;
You could well strike me, I believe at heart ;
God help me that am troubled with you so !
Feel both hands now ; the blood 's alive there, beats
And flutters in the fingers and the palms.

 Bouch. True, hot enough ; what will you do ? the king
Comes back to take farewell and hold his way
With some thin train that gathers Londonwards ;
Thence ere he take ship shall my lord make way
Among the westward alder-meadows, thrust
Between soft Godstow poplars and warm grass
Right into Woodstock and pleached rose-places ;
Shall the queen follow lest he lack a face
For welcome, and sweet words to kiss i' the lip ?
I would go with you lest some harm should fall.

 Qu. El. No need, for would God let them hurt me ?
  Well,
I would fain see the rose grow, Robert.

 Bouch.   Being fair,
A woman is worth pains to see.

 Qu. El.   Being fair.
Sweet stature hath she and fair eyes, men say ;
I am but black, with hair that keeps the braid,
And my face hurt and bitten of the sun
Past medicine of all waters ; so his tooth
Bites hard in France, and strikes the brown grape hot,
Makes the wine leap, no skin-room spares for white, —
I know well now ; the woman has that white,

His water-weed, his golden girl-flower
With lank sapped stem and green rind moist at core. `
Ay, gold ! but no crown's gold to all this hair,
That 's hard, my Robert.

    Bouch.   See how men will lie ;
They call you hard, this people, sour to bite ;
Now I will trust your sweetness, do but say
You will not touch her if I get you through.

    Qu. El. I will not hurt her, Bouchard ;. for God's
      love,
Help me ; I swear by God I will not hurt,
I will not — Ah, sweet Robert, bear me through,   ·
Do not make smiles and never move your mouth :
When we ride back I will do anything,
Wear man's dress, take your horse to water, — yea,
Kiss clean your feet of any travelling dust, —
Yea, what your page has never done I will
For mere love, Robert, for pure love of you ;
Nay, if I meant to stab or poison her,
You might so chide me, Bouchard, bid me back,
Not now ! I will not hurt her ; there again.
Kiss me ! I love you as a man loves God !
Be sorry for me !

    Bouch.   Ah well, well; no doubt
But my Lord wrought me with a tender hand,
Spoiled half a man in making; there, sit, sit.
I felt your teeth come through that bitter kiss.
Sit now and talk ; it is my service, madam,

A man's good service merely, nothing else,
To ride for you, to ride with you, — not more.

    Qu. El. I have some help yet of this Bouchard, then?
See now, sir, you are knight and gentleman;
I pray you that your service fail not here.
For wears a man rich office and rich name
Nearer than wife about him? so the king
Wears me; and so I bid you serve him, sir.
I bid you? ,rather I take prayer to me
And catch your faith with prayer; right meek I am,
Chide with me, Bouchard, if I be not meek;
No child was ever so milk-mouthed, no bird
That picks out seed from scented and pink palms.
To say soft words is seasonable; and good
To think of all men smoothly; else a sin
May sting you suddenly — as him it stung —
Hell's heat burn through that whorish mouth of hers!

    Bouch. Madam!

    Qu. El.   And God that knows I weep!

    Bouch.   Keeps count
(The monks' song says it) of your flitting times,
Seals all your tears up safely, doth he not?
Hark, there's one singing.

    Qu. El.   But no monk this time.
Look, in the garden by the red wall's turn,
The king's fool under covert, and steals fruit;
Pluck such raw pears and spoil so bad a song,
That breaks my patience; a lewd witch-burden!

One sings outside : —

This was written in God's name ;
    The Devil kissed me
Mouth on mouth with little shame
    Under a big tree.
He fed me full with good meat,
    The best there might be ;
He gave me black wine and sweet
Red fruit and honey-meal to eat ;
    Domine, laudamus te.

He made straight the lame
    And fat he made me ;
So he gat good game,
    Kisses three by three.
He was shapen like a carl,
    A swine's foot had he ;
Like a dog's his mouth did snarl,
His hands were foul with loam and marl;
    Domine, laudamus te.

Qu. El. Eh, what lewd words so mutter in his teeth ?
I hear no good ones ; bid them see him whipped.

Outside : —

A bat came out of heaven
    That had a flat snout ;
A loaf withouten leaven,
    Crumbs thereof fell out ;

The Devil thrust up with his thumb,
    Said tho to me,
Lo you, there shall be left no crumb
When I and you in heaven come ;
    Domine, laudamus te.

There were many leavés thick
    Grown well over me ;
A big branch of a little stick
    Is this greené tree ;
He showed me brave things to wear,
    Pleasant things to see ;
A good game had we twain there,
The leavés weren broad and fair ;
    Domine, laudamus te.

Qu. El. Bid the grooms whip him ; even a dog like that
Can be a fret to me, a thorn-prick.   Ah,
Such beasts as feed about us, and we make
Communion of their breath !   I am sick at him.
Why, my sweet friend, I pray you of your love
Do me some service.
    Bouch.   Nay, the fool 's no harm ;
Let be a little ; service was your word ?
See now, he creeps by nodding his fool's head,
With back and shoulders rounded for the sun ;
Let the poor beast be ; 't is no worse than dogs
When the rain makes them howl, soaks to the bone

As he is sodden through the wits of him.
Now, sweet, sit closer, talk with me ; you said
Service ? what service must I do ? the king,
It's the king has me at his heels, a dog
For service ; the best work one does for love ;
As I do service for my lord the king.

    Qu. El. Ay, for you love him ; I have learnt you, sir,
Can say my Bouchard through and turn the leaf.
Are you his servant, lackey, chattel, purse,
The sheath where he's the hilt ? you love him ; eh ?

    Bouch. Service and love make lordship stable ; well,,
Suppose I love him ; there be such about
As would stoop shoulder and fit knee to bear
Worse weight than I do, only for pure love, —
Clean love, that washes out so much !

    Qu. El.   Ah, sir,
They make you laugh, then ?

    Bouch.   Well, not loud ; a brush
That strikes one's lips with laughter as a fly
Touches a fruit and drops clean off, you see.
Men love so, pay them wages (ah, not gold,
No gold of course, but credit, name, safe room,
Broad space to sun the back and cram the sides
And shake fat elbows and grow longer beards, —
There's all one wants, now) pay them such, I say —
Lo, sir, our friend hath never wrought for that,
That he should take it ; love holds otherwhere
Than by the purfled corners of your sleeve,

Eats no such food as keeps your pages warm
Nor wears such raiment.

Qu. El.   Ay, my Bouchard, so ?
I 've measure of you somewhere ; why serve me ?
Why sweat and crawl to get me such a rose
And save my gloves one thorn ?

Bouch.   Nay, I know not ;
Find some clean reason for a miry foot
Or tell me why God makes the sun get up
Pricked out like a tame beast, I 'll answer you
Why I am pleased to be so serviceable.
But why our friend's lip tastes a sweet therein
Who serves for honesty ? this were more hard to say.
Still the truth stands, he 'll work some three good hours
Outside your hireling ; yea, that 's much for him ;
And all to get such dog's wage as a rag
To wrap some naked wound's unseemliness
Caught serving you, lest the sight turn your blood
And swell your sick throat out at him.

Qu. El.   No more ?
I doubt you do belie both sides of love.

Bouch. But ask him rather ; there 's Jean Becqueval,
King Louis has him throttled up in steel
That was a strong knight once, and had broad bones
To get the mail shut over, not so tight.
A keen sword, madam, makes blunt work in time,
For this man struck two blows for you or three
Some years back, when your courtiers snarled and spat ;

Who might have children beat him on his mouth
And could not shake about the chin for spite
To save their plucking at his beard.   Poor fool,
I dare well say he hates you not the least,
Most like would bite now for you with his teeth,
Since both hands could not pull the scabbard straight
Or loose the band o' the visor and not let
The steel snap on his fingers.

   Qu. El.   If you say truth,
I swear by God's blood I am shamed in it,
Shamed out of face ; but I misdoubt you lie
Your old hard way, lie perfectly.   Be good,
Say you did lie.

   Bouch.   I have said short of truth.
Nay, now you find this wound in him of yours,
Should you fall weeping ? ask our lord so much ;
He 'll swear by God's face, finger his own beard,
And twist a hawk's foot round or hurt its neck,
And say by God such things are pitiful.
Come, is your friend less pinched for his good will ?
You know he would not, set things broadly down,
Sweep this cast up and leave him room to throw,
Change his soiled coat to be set clean in gold ;
He would just choose to serve you his best way
Something beyond my warrant.   Why, in France
Last March the king's friend, Guerrat of Sallières,
— A good knight, — has that long mouth like a toad's,
And eats a woman like a grape with it, —

(Spits the husk out I mean and strains the core)
Spake thus to me: "Sir Robert, there 's a man
Lies flat with rust upon his lips to chew
Who while your Queen touched Paris with her feet
Would have plucked out his hairs for cushion-stuff
To save her shoes a sprinkle of weak rain, —
Burnt out his eyes a-sputter in the head
If she misliked their color."

 Qu. El.   Not Sallières?

 Bouch. It was my question; at which word thrown out
His head went sideways as a big fish flaps
And shoves with head and body, showing white
I' the black oil of sea-water before storm
(You take such off-shore with sides weltering)
And the cheeks got quick twinkles of eased flesh
And the chin laughed: " By Mary's hand," he said,
" I think I would not."

 Qu. El.   Ah, the fool he was!
Is he grown fat? he must be fat by this.

 Bouch. I held to him; what name and ways and work,
Where the man hid; whereat my Guerrat rolls
And chatters, — " By the milk of Pilate's nurse
And by the sleeve that wiped king Herod's beard,
I hope the place be something worse than hell,
Or I shall fare the worse next world, by God!"

 Qu. El. What noise runs towards us? is the king past
     Thames
Think you, by this? — Take this one word of me;

Albeit I lay no heavy thought on it
Lest pain unmake me, hold this truth of mine,
Sir Robert, which your swordsmen and blank wits,
I doubt, would feel for half one's life and miss;
I had sooner fare as doth this Becqueval
Than as I fare; yea, if a man will weep,
Let him weep here. God is no good to me,
Nor any man i' the world; I have no love
And no smooth hour in those twelve pricks of plague
That smite my blood each once a day. Nay, go;
Do me some greeting to my lord. Farewell.

> [*Exit* BOUCHARD.

I shall find time to hate you; yea, I do
Hate him past speech. Let me just cool my head
And gather in some breath to face the king —
I am quite stilled.

> *Enter* King HENRY.

> Fair days upon my lord.

K. Hen. How does the queen? — Three, — not four
> provinces
To shut one's hand on. — Are you well? — next month
My face at Paris and his hands in mine
Touch service; two, three provinces at most;
I must have more.

Qu. El.   I thank you, well enough.
How doth my Paris? — That means ill to me,
That beat of his two fingers on the cheek.
Will Bouchard make no liar, does one know?

K. Hen. Fair news ; our Louis to the throat in steel,
And cannot clear his saddle at a leap,
But slips and sticks there as he did years back,
Not in the saddle, but across a bed
His feet in time drew clear of and made room.

 Qu. El. Made room for you to slide between and thrust
Across the pillows with a sideways head
To warm about the corner where his feet
Were thrust out late ; so God keep heat for it
To please you always !

 K. Hen.   Ay, not best at swords,
Good Louis ; I was eased with swinging steel
In thick fields under lusty months of sun ;
He would play blind, wring back my hand in his,
Fall in hard thought.   But see now ; have I not
A dozen French heads broken through the neck
Hung at my sleeve here, madam, threes and threes ?
Guy d'Héricourt and Guerrat of Sallières,
Denis of Gordes, Peter of the March,
I have their tongues shut with gold coins of mine
To seal the lips back ; Jacques Becqueval
Shows teeth to nibble ; if these fail me quite,
I 'll say we have played at luck with God and lost
By some trick's foil; being no such fools of his
As chew the lazy purpose with their teeth,
Eat and wax full and laugh till hair falls out ;
Why, all the world lives without sleeping-whiles,
God makes and mars and turns not weak one whit,

But we must find some roost to perch and blink
And wag thick chins at the world ; I hate all men
That have large faces with dead eyes in them
And good full fronts of fool

Qu. El.　　　　　　　　Am I worth words ?

K. Hen. So quick, so quick ! are you true wife to me ?

Qu. El. I praise God for it, how loyal I have lived
Your soul shall answer.

K. Hen.　　　　　　　What, I see the blood
That goes about the heart and makes you hot, —
French blood, south blood ! I would not tax you far,
But spare my Louis ; he did no such wrong
As I did when I let you slip my hand
In a new French glove you had sewn with gold.

Qu. El. This is a courteous holiness of yours
That smites so in my face ; have you not heard
Of men whose swervéd feet lie delicate
In common couches, with beds made to them
Where priests shed no fair water ?　Nay, this breath
You chide me with makes treason to your breath
That was my promise ; if I be your wife,
The unclean witness of my well-doing
Is your own sin.

K. Hen.　　　　　This is a fevered will
That you seem drunk withal.

Qu. El.　　　　　　　　　I bond-broken ?
You lay your taint my way ; blush now a little,
Pay but some blood ; do but defend yourself ;

It is a double poison in revolt
When it deserts the bare rebellion
To be half honest.

K. Hen. You are not wise.

Qu. El. I would not:
For wisdom smites awry, when foolishness
Keeps the clean way.

K. Hen. Have you done yet with me?

Qu. El. I thrust your bags out with round cheeks of gold
That were my people's ; thickened with men the sides
Of your sick, lean, and barren enterprise ;
Made capable the hunger of your state
With subsidies of mine own fruitfulness ;
Enriched the ragged ruin of your plans
With purple patched into the serge and thread
Of your low state ; you were my pensioner ;
There 's not a taste of England in your breath
But I did pay for.

K. Hen. Better I had never seen you
Than wear such words unchallenged. You are my wife ;
I would the name were lost with mine to it.
I put no weight upon you of the shame
That is my badge in you ; the carriage of it
Pays for your gold.

Qu. El. Ay, you will tax not me,
Being made so whole of your allegiance, you,
Perfect as patience? why, the cause, this cause
(Be it what you say, — but saying it you lie,

Are simply liar, my lord!) the shame would prick
A very dog to motion of such blood
As takes revenge for the shame done, the shame
I' the body, in the sufferance of a blow, —
But you are patient.

K. Hen.   I will not find your sense.

Qu. El. Nay, I think so; when you do understand,
Praise me a little then.   For this time, sir,
I have no such will to trouble you; and here,
Even here shall leave-taking atone us twain;
Therefore farewell.   When I am dead, my lord,
I pray you praise me for my sufferance;
You see I chide not; nay, I say no word;
I will put seals like iron on my mouth
Lest it revolt at me, or any shame
Push some worse phrase in than "God keep you, sir." [*Exit.*

K. Hen. I am her fool; no word to get her dumb?
I am like the tales of Cornish Mark long since,
To be so baffled.   Well, being this way eased,
I need not see her anger twice i' the eyes ·   ·
Get me a hawk to ride with presently.   [*Exit.*

9*

III. *At Woodstock.*

Rosamond.

B ELLE est madame, et bien douce en son dire ;
  Dieu lui fit don de pleurer ou de rire
Plus doucement que femme qui soupire
        Et puis oublie.

Bonne est madame, et me baise de grace ;
Bien me convient baiser si belle face,
Bien me convient que si doux corps embrasse
        Et plus n'oublie.

Blonde est madame, ayant de tristes yeux ;
Entre or et roux Dieu fit ses longs cheveux ;
Bien mal me fait, si l'en aime bien mieux,
        Et moins oublie.

Blanche est madame et gracieuse à voir ;
Ne sais si porte en corps azur ou noir ;
Que m'a donné sa belle bouche avoir
        Jamais n'oublie.

I bade them tell you I was sick ; the sun
Pains me.   Sit here.
    K. Hen.   There 's no sick show in you.
Sing still, and I will sit against your feet

And see the singing measure in your throat
Moved evenly ; the headband leaves your hair
Space to lie soft outside.

 Ros.   Stoop then and touch
That I may bind it on your hands ; I would
Fain have such hands to use so royally.
As you are king, sir, tell me without shame
Doth not your queen share praise with you, show best
In all crowned ways even as you do ? I have heard
Men praise the state in her and the great shape ;
Yet pray you, though you find her sweet enow,
Praise her not over-measure ; yet speak truth ;
But so I would not have you make her praise
The proper pleasure of your lips, the speech
Found best in them ; yet do not scant her so
That I may see you tender of my pain,
Sparing to gall my wits with laud of her.

 K. Hen. O sweet, what sting is this she makes in you ?
A Frenchwoman, black-haired and with gray lips
And fingers like a hawk's cut claw that nips
One's wrist to carry — is this so great a thing
As should wring wet out of your lids ?

 Ros.   I know
That for my sake you pinch her praises in,
Starve her of right ; do not so fearfully ;
I shall best love you if you praise her, seeing
I would not have you marry a worse face,
Say, than mine even ; therefore be liberal,

Praise her to the full, till you shall see that I
Fall sick upon your words, bid them be pitiful
And bruise not me.

K. Hen.   I will not praise her to you.
Show me a little golden good of yours,
But some soft piece of gracious habit grown
.Common with you, quite new with me and sweet.
It is the smell of roses where you come
That makes my sense faint now ; you taste of it,
Walk with it always.

Ros.   Hark, the rain begins,
Slips like a bird that feels among shut leaves ;
One — two ; it catches in the rose-branches
Like a word caught.   Now, as I shut your eyes,
Show me what sight gets first between the lids,
So covered in to make false witness true.
Speak, and speak faith.

K. Hen.   I think this first ; here once
The hard noon being too strong a weight for us,
We lay against the edges of slant leaves
Facing the grass, our bodies touching them,
Cooled from the sun, and drank cold wine ; you had
A straight gown flaked with gold i' the undersleeves ;
And in your throat I caught the quick faint red
Drunk down, that ran and stained it out of white,
A long warm thread not colored like a vein
But wine-colored ; this was a joy to see.
O little throat so tender to show red,

Would you not wear my lips as well, be kissed
To a soft mark if one but touched you so?
I will not touch; only to feel you fast,
Lie down and take your feet inside both hands,
Untie your hair to blind both eyes across —
Yea, there sweet, kiss me now.
    Ros.   Do but stoop yet
And I will put my fingers where the hair
Is mixed upon the great crown's wearing-place;
Sir, do you think I must fall old indeed
First of us two? look how between my wrists
Even about the purplest seat of them
This lean scant flesh goes in. I am grown past love;
The breath aches each way in my sobbing sides
When I would sing, and tears climb up my throat
In bitter breaks like swellings of round fruit
From the rind inwards, and my pulses go
Like fits of singing when the head gives way
And leaves pure naught to stammer in spoilt lips,
Even for this and my sad patience here
Built up and blinded in with growing green,
Use me not with your eyes untenderly,
But though I tire you, make you sigh at me,
Say no blame overloud; I have flowers only
And foolish ways to get me through the day,
And songs of yours to piece with weeping words
And famish and forget. Pray you go now,
I am the abuse of your compassion.

K. Hen. I am gone presently ; but for this space
Give me poor leave to love you with mine eyes
And feasted expectation of shut lips.
God help ! your hair burns me to see like gold
Burnt to pure heat ; your color seen turns in me
To pain and plague upon the temple-vein
That aches as if the sun's heat snapt the blood
In hot mid measure ; I could cry on you
Like a maid weeping-wise, you are so fair
It hurts me in the head, makes the life sick
Here in my hands, that one may see how beats
Feverous blue upon my finger-tips.
Touch me now gently ; I am as he that saith
In the great song sick words and sorrowful
Of love's hard sweet and hunger of harsh hours ;
Your beauty makes me blind and hot, I am
Stabbed in the brows with it.

    Ros.   Yea, God be good,
Am I fair yet ? but say that I am fair,
Make me assured, praise me quite perfectly
Lest I doubt God may love me something less
And his hot fear so nip me in the cheek
That I burn through. Nay, but go hence ; I would
Even lose the sweet I love, that I may lose
The fear of losing it.

    K. Hen.   I am gone quickly.
You know my life is made a pain to me
With angry work, harsh hands upon my life

That finger in the torn sad sides of it
For the old thorn; touch but my face and feel
How all is thwarted with thick networking
Where your lips found it smooth, clung soft; there, now,
You take some bruise and gall of mine clear out
With a cool kissing mouth.

   Ros.   I had a will
To make some chafing matter with your pride
And laugh at last; ay, also to be eased
Of some small wrath at your harsh tarriance;
But you put sadness softly in my lips
With your marred speech. Look, the rain slackens yet.

   K. Hen. I will go now that both our hearts are sweet
And lips most peaceable; so shall we sleep
Till the next honey please them, with a touch
Soft in our mouths; sing once and I am gone.

   Ros. I will sing something heavy in the word
That it may serve us; help me to such words.
The marigolds have put me in my song,
They shine yet redly where you made me it.

     Hélas, madame, ayez de moi merci,
     Qui porte en cœur triste fleur de souci;
     N'est plus de rose, et plus ne vois ici
          Que triste fleur.

     M'est trop grand deuil, hélas, dans cette vie;
     Car vieil espoir me lie et me délie,
     Et triste fleur m'est force, ô belle amie,
          Porter en cœur.

See the rain ! have you care to ride by this ?
Yea, kiss me one strong kiss out of your heart,
Do not kiss more ; I love you with my lips,
My eyes and heart, your love is in my blood,
I shall die merely if you hold to me.

IV. *Ante-Chapel at Shene. Choir-music from within.
In the passage outside,* ARTHUR, *a boy of the choir,
reading.*

Enter SIR ROBERT DE BOUCHARD.

Bouchard.

S HE spares me time to think of it ; well, so
    I pull this tumbled matter square with God,
What sting can men's mouths hurt me with ?   What harm
Because the savor of undieted sense
Palates not me ? the taste and smell of love
Sickens me, being so fed with its keen use
That delicate divisions of soft touch
Feel gross to me as dullest accident ?
That way of will most men take pleasure in
It tires my feet to walk.   Then for the harder game, —
Joust where the steel swings, fight that clears up blood,
I want the relish too ; being no such sinewed ape,
Blunder of brawn and jolted muscle-work,
As beats and bleeds about his iron years,

Anoints his hide with stupid lust and sleep,
Fattens to mould and dies ; rubs sides with dust,
Ending his riddle. I have seen time enough,
Struck blows and tricked and paid and won and wrought,
I know not well why wrought. A monk, now — there 's
    right work ;
Dull work or wise, body and head keep up ;
I should have pulled in scapular and alb
To shut my head up and its work, who knows ?
    Arthur (outside). They told me I should see the king
    come in ;
I shall not get the words out clear enough, —
No time, I doubt. I wonder will he wear
Chain-mail or samite-work ? I would take mail, —
A man fares best in good close joints of mail.
Fautor, — I seem to catch it up their way ;
This time I 'll come off clear yet. One rhyme sticks —

    (He repeats.)
Fautor meus, magne Deus, quis adversùm tibi stabit ?
Parùm ridet qui te videt ; sponsam sponsus accusabit ;
Sicut herbam qui superbam flatu gentem dissipabit,
Flectit cœlum quasi velum quo personam implicabit.

There, all straight out, clean forthright singing, this ;
I 'll see the king in the face and speak out hard
That he shall hear me. Last time all fell wrong ;
I had that song about the lily-plants

Growing up goodly in their green of time
With gold heads and gold sprinkles in the neck
And God among them, feeding like a lamb
That takes out sin ; so I let slip his name, —
Euh ! I can touch the prints of the big switch ;
One, six, twelve, — ah ! the sharp small suckers stung
Like a whole hive loose, as Hugh's arm swung out.
Good for this king that I shall see to have
Fine padded work and silk seats pillow-puft
Instead of wood to twist on painfully.

    Bouch. So comes mine answer in ; I thank you, Lord ;
I 'll none of this. Give men clean work and sleep,
And baby bodies this priest's blessed way.
But, being so set between the time's big jaws
To dodge and keep me from the shut o' the teeth,
Shuffle from lip to lip, a shell with priest
For kernel in the husk and rind of knight, —
No chink bit in me, but nigh swallowed whole, —
Who says my trick that, played on either, makes
Music for me and sets my head on work,
Is devil's lesson ? Pity that lives by milk
Suckles not me ; I see no reason set
To keep me from the general use of things
Which no more holds the great regard of man
Than children spoiling flies. Respect and habit
Find no such tongue against me ; I but wear
The raiment of my proper purpose, not
The threadworn coat of use. Even who keeps on

Such garments for the reputation's want,
Wears them unseamed inside. The boy there now —
Arth. Yea, I loathe Hugh. Peter he beat, and me, —
Me twice, because that day the queen came in
I twisted back my head to thrust well through
The carved work's double lattice to get sight
Of a tall woman with gold clothes and hair
That shone beyond her clothes; so sharp he smote,
The grim beast Hugh with boarish teeth and hair
All his chin long and where no hair should be!
And Peter pinched and pushed all vespers through
To get my turn and see her. How she went
Holding her throat up, with her round neck out
Curdwhite, no clot in it not smooth to stroke, —
All night I shook in sleep for that one thing,
Stirred with my feet and pulled about awry.
I think too she kept smiling with her mouth
(Her wonderful red quiet mouth) and prayed
All to herself. Now that men call a mouth, —
And Hugh's begrimed big lips you call the same
That make a thick smile up with all their fat
Never but when he gets one by the nape
To make him sprawl and weep. How all the hair
Drew the hard shining of the candle-fires
And shone back harder with a flare in it
Through all the plaits and bands. Then Hugh said, —
        "Look,
You Arthur, that white woman with such eyes

Is worṣe in hell than any devil that seethes ;
She keeps the color of it in her hair
That shakes like flame so.   Wait till I get in
And teach the beast's will in your female flesh
With some red slits in it, to get out loose
In such dog's ways."   But Hugh lied hard, I think ;
For he said after in his damned side-room   .
· What fierce account God made of such a name
And how the golden king that made God songs
Chid at their ways and called them this and that ;
And he loved many queens with just such hair ·
And such good eyes, and had more scores of them
Than I have stripes since last red week on me.
So I can see Hugh lied.   For no Jew's wife
Looked ever so, or found such ways to hold
Her sweet straight body. — But my next, — that 's hard.

(*Reads.*)

Bouch. Yea, there the snakè's head blinks ? yea, doth
it there ?
O this sweet thorn that worries the kind flesh !
.Yea, but the devil's seedling side-graft, Lord,
That pinches out the sap. — I 'll talk to him.

Enter from the Chapel QUEEN ELEANOR.

Qu. El. Ah, you here, Bouchard? is it well with you
When you hear music?   I am hot i' the face ;
Kiss me now, Robert, where the red begins,
And tell me, does no music hurt you ?   Ah, —
Will no man stop them ?

Bouch.   Speak me lower then ;
No time to kiss bad words out on the mouth
As one treads flame out with the heel.   Well were it,
That you should keep the purpose in your lips
From knowledge of your eyes ; let none partake,
No inquisition of the air get out
One secret, or the imperious sun compel
One word of you.   Wisdom doth sheathe her hand
To smite the fool behind.

Qu. El.   I pray you, sir,
Let be your sentence ; O, I am sick to death,
Could lie down here and bruise my head with stone,
Cover up hands and feet and die at once.
Nathless I will not have her eyes and hair
Crown-circled, and her breasts embraced with gold,
When the grave catches me.   It is mere time,
The mere sick fault of age I limp with ; yea,
Time was I had put such fierce occasion on
Like a new scented glove ; but now this thing
Tastes harsh as if I drank that blood indeed
Which I 'll not even have spilled in dust ; it clings,
Under the lip, makes foul the sense, — ha, there,
I knew that noise was close upon my head.

   Arthur (*outside*).
Matrem pater, fratrem frater, iste condemnabit eum;
Erit nemo quem postremo tu non incusabis reum;
Nihil tactum quod non fractum; fulgor ibit ante Deum;
Mea caro prodest rarò; non est laudi caput meum.

Qu. El. Say now you love me, Robert ; I fear God,
Fear is more bitter than a hurt worm's tooth,
But if God lets one love me this side heaven
And puts his breath not out, then shall I laugh
I' the eyes of him for mere delight, pluck off
Fear that ties man to patience, white regret,
All mixture of diseaséd purpose, made
To cut the hand at wrist ; remorse and doubt
Shall die of want in me.

    Bouch.   Too much of this ;
Get your eyes back. Think how some ten days gone
He drew loose hair into his either hand
And how the speech got room between their mouths
Only to breathe in and go out ; at times,
How she said " Eleanor " to try the name,
Found not so sweet as Rosamond to say ;
Perhaps too, " Love, the Frenchwoman gets thin,
Her mouth is something older than her hair ;
Count by these petals, pluck them three and three,
What months it takes to rid the sun of her,
And make some grave-grass wealthier " ; will you bear
This ?

    Qu. El. Do men tie the sword this way, or that ?
Were I a knight now I would gird it on `
Strained hard upon the clasp, would feel the hilt
Bruise my side blue and work the stamp therein
Deep as blood hides i' the flesh. I love pain well to feel;
As to wring in one's fingers, — the least pain ;

It kills the hard impatience of the soul,
Cools heat of head, makes bearable all shame
That finds a work to do ; yea, very sense
Tastes it for comfort, gets assured with it,
Being strong to smite the flesh, and wear pain well.
She must hate pain, that woman ; it should jar
Her thin soft sense through, tear it up like silk ;
What, if worms eat me that sweet flesh in time ?

Arthur (outside).

Motu mentis quasi ventis facit maria levari;
Ex avenâ flatu plenâ facit dulcem sonum dari;
Tument colles quasi folles quia jussit exsufflari,
Et quæ deplet manu replet labra calicis amari.

Qu. El. Ay, bitter ; for it bites and burns one through
As the sharp sting of wine curdles the mouth.
He would not wed her if I died ? I know, —
A laugh with all his teeth in it, the beard
So twisted from the underlip about, —
Eh, said he that he would not marry her ?
Bouch. Nay, but who deemed else ? no man certainly.
When the weak lust falls dead and eyeless flesh
Is as a beast asleep and sick of meat, ·
What marvel if no spirit there holds out ?
No appetite, that like the unchilded sea
(In whose unprofitable and various womb
Fair ships lie sidelong with a fisher's buoy

Miles down in water) hungers for such orts
As riot spares lean want, is yet so wide,
So vast of ravin or so blind in scope,
As can abide the chewed and perished meats
That relish died upon.   Fill famine to the lips,
The word of bread shall turn his throat awry;
So doth the sense of love all love put out,
And kiss it from that very place o' the soul
Mere wish made sweet indeed.

    Qu. El.   I am sorry for you;
This foolish poison in your tongue forgets
All better things to say.

    Bouch.   It is dull truth;
This gift found in me should much profit you.   .

    Qu. El.   I care not for you; I could wish you hanged
But for some love that sticks here in my head,
Some stupid trick caught up, — like play with straws,
Tune-burden twisted over in sick ears
That keeps up time with fever; so habit fools me
To use you like a friend.

    Bouch.   It is a piteous thing
When honesty grown gray has hairs plucked out
By such unreverent fingers.   Come, let be;
I marvel what lewd matter jars your talk
So much past tune.

    Qu. El.   'T is better talk than do
Where doing means actual harm.   Perchance this thing
Shall trap our souls indeed, — eh?

Bouch.   Doubt me not;
I think so truly.   Prithee let us in,
Wash hands and weep.
Qu. El.   You have marred my will to prayer.
God is right gracious, may be he shall help,
As we do honorably.   I will not go.

Arthur (*outside*).

Multo fletu non expletu facit teneras pupillas;
Dente tangi, manu frangi jubet nitidas mamillas;
Quum amœnæ parum genæ nudas exhibent maxillas,
Fiet gravis odor suavis si quis osculabit illas.

Qu. El. Who made that hymn?
Bouch.   Aloys of Blois.
Qu. El.   Ah priest!
You should be priest, my Bouchard, scalp and mouth,
You have such monk's ways.   If she be foul to God
And her sweet breath ill savor in his lip,
Then shall her blood-spilling be sacrifice
And cleanse us in the blow.   I do thank God,
I praise the wording of his prayer, will make
Fast and sweet words and thereto thanksgiving,
Be married to his love, my purpose making
Such even wing and way with his.
Bouch.   Yea, first
Show me the perfect fashion of her death.
Qu. El. What fashion? feel this flasket next my waist,

10

Full to the wicked lips, crammed up and full
With drugs and scents that touch you in the mouth
And burn you all up, face and eyes at once, —
They say so; they may lie, who knows ? but kill
The thing does really; do you kiss me now ?

    Bouch. Some Frenchman gave my queen the thing to
      keep ?

    Qu. El. I wot well England would not give a queen
Six grains of salt she paid in salt of tears.
France makes good blood, made Becqueval and me;
I bade him get me for love's sake, — years gone, —
Such mortal matter. Ah, poor Becqueval,
A good time had we in that pleasance-walk;
I with few dames about the white pear-trees, —
Spring was it ? yea, for green sprang thick as flame
And the birds bit the blossom and sang hard, —
Now sat and tore up flowers to waste, wet strips
Of hyacinth, rain-sodden bells, — then stood
To make them braid my running hair well back,
Pluck out the broken plait of March-lilies,
Lest one should mutter, — " Ha, the queen comes late,
Her hair unwoven and cheeks red as though
Fingers and lips had kissed and fondled them, —
Ay, pity of her ! " so for that, — what words
I choke with saying !

    Bouch.   Weak in words indeed ;
See how I shut them back upon the mouth.
The king comes here to chapel ; let us hence.

Qu. El. I am very ready. Nay, this turn it is;
I am so free and pleasant of my mood,
I can scarce go for simple joyousness.   [*Exeunt.*

Arthur (*outside*).

Pater, e me mendas deme, fac ut cingar prece suavi ;
Pater, e me vinum premi, fac ut purgar fæce gravi ;
Tu me bonis imple donis ut implentur melle favi,
Tu me rege tuâ lege, quia mundum non amavi.

V. *At Woodstock.*

Rosamond.

L ATE summer now, but in the fair blue spring
    How shall God bear me ? Once (men say) Lord
      Christ
Walked between rivers in his rose-garden
With some old saint who had a wife by him
To feed with apple-pulp and honeycomb,
A wife like Mary in king David's time
Long after, — but a snake so stung his foot
He came back never, being lame at heél.
A story some priest wrote out all in gold,
Painting the leaves green, for a king to read ;
But the king burnt it ; whom God therefore took
And sold him to some Turk, with eyes thrust out.

Here in my garden, now his feet are healed
From those twin stains where bit the hanging-nails,
He would not come to let me kiss them whole,
Wash them with oil and wet fruits bruised to juice,
Rare waters stained and scented through with rose, —
Though my hair be as long as Magdalen's,
As yellow, may be. Mine eyes and eyelids ache,
Too thick to see past, weeping swells them blue ;
And the veins narrow visibly and waste
Where next the elbow neither hand could span ;
The flesh that wore glad color is gone gray,
And soon the hair will ; yea, not milk but blood
Fills my breast through, not good for any child
To lay sweet lips to ; I am as a gold cup
With beaten edges and dry mouths of dust,
That tears weep into, and that cunning man
By whose wit I was fashioned lets them run
And lets men break me. If I were well dead,
Then were the tears all spilled over the ground
And I made empty ; also I pray God
To get me broken quickly ; else, who knows,
If I live long till these years too seem gray
As a flower ruined, then ere sleep at night
I shall be grown too stark and thin to pray,
Nor will God care to set me praying then.
Maids will keep round me, girls with smooth warm hair
When mine is hard, no silk in it to feel, —
Tall girls to dress me, laughing underbreath,
Too low for gold to tighten at the waist.

Eh, the hinge sharpens at the grate across?
Five minutes now to get the green walk through
And turn, — the chestnut leaves will take his hair
If he turn quick ; or I shall hear some bud
Fall, or some pebble's clink along the fence
Or stone his heel grinds, or torn lime-blossom
Flung at me from behind ; not poppies now
Nor marigolds, but rose and lime-flower.

Enter QUEEN ELEANOR.

Qu. El. (*to Bouchard within*). Outside, — outside, — I bade
    you keep outside ;
Look to her people ; tell me not of shame ;
Look to her women.

Ros.   Ah God ! shall this be so ?

Qu. El. I 'll have no man at hand to help her through ;
Not till the king be come ; tush, tell not me,
No treaties — talk of promises, you talk !
I will not strike her ; look to them ; Lord God !
I bade you have a heed ; there, go now ; there ! —
Here, golden lady, look me in the face ;
Give me both hands, that I may read you through,
See how the blood runs, how the eyes take light,
How the mouth sets when one is beautiful.
Ah sweet, and shall not men praise God for you ?

Ros. I shall die now. Madam, you are the queen.

Qu. El. Does fear so speak ?

Ros.   Not so ; for pain with me

Is a worn garment or that common food
That sleep comes after best; what wrath will do
I make no reckoning with.

   Qu. El.   What love hath done
I keep the count of; did he not hold this way?
Did you not set both hands behind his head,
And curl your body like a snake's? not set
Each kiss between the hair of lip and chin,
Cover your face upon his knees, draw down
His hands on you, shut either eye to kiss?
Then it was " Love, a gold band either side,
A gold ring to pull close each knot of hair ! "
" Nay, not so ; kiss me rather like a bird
That lets his bill cut half the red core through
And rend and bite for pleasure, — eh ! I felt
What pinched my lips up after " ; — was it not ?
Did it not sting i' the blood, pluck at the breath
If a bird caught his song up in the leaves ?
Eh ! this was sweet too, that you called the king
Some girl's name with no royal note in it
To spoil the chatter, — some name like a kiss
The lips might loose and hesitate upon ?
He would weave up this yellow skein of yours
To knot and ravel, though his hands might pluck
Some plait a little overmuch ; your throat,
Pure pearl, too fair to swell or strain with sobs,
One would not have a rough thing rasp it round,
Not steel to touch it, only soft warm silk.

Will you not sing now, loose your hair well out
For me to hold the gracious weft? Alas,
So white you grow, love ; the head drops indeed,
A moan comes out of that kissed mouth of yours !
You harlot, are you sick to look at me ?
Though my heel bruise you in the gold snake's head
I choke to touch you.

 Ros.   I shall die without.
But give me time to speak; wherefore am I
That am made soft in this my body's strength
And in my soul smooth and affectionate
So taken in your loathing ? you do not right
To hate me that am harmless ; see my face,
You will not smite me afterwards ; this sin
Was not begot of wilfulness in me
To be your pain and a shame burning you ;
Yea verily, no evil will or wit
Made me your traitor; there came not in my mind
One thought to gall you past good patience ; yea,
If you could see the pained poor heart in me
You would find nothing hateful toward you
In all the soft red record its blood makes.

 Qu. El. Thou art more fool than thief ; I have not seen
A beaten beast so humble of its mouth,
So shaming me as you ; I am ashamed
That such a thing can see me in the eyes.
You do not think that I shall let you go
Being well caught ? Ah harlot, have you made

Thief's japes at me, lewd guesses on my wrath,
Spat towards me ? and now God gives me you
I shall play soft and touch you with my gloves,
Nay, make my lips two kissing friends of yours
Because mere love and a sweet fault i' the flesh
Put you to shame ?   Look, you shall die for that,
Because you sinned not out of hate to me
That have and hate you. ,Do not shake at it,
I will not strike you yet ; what hands are mine
To take such hangman's matter to their work
And be clean after ? but a charm I have
Quick to undo God's cunning weft of flesh
And mix with deadly waters the glad blood
That hath so pure a sense and subtleness.
This is a gracious death made out for you
And praiseworthy ; you shall die no base way,
Seeing what king's lips have fastened in your neck.
Choose me this edge to try your flesh upon
That feels so precious — like a holy thing
Kissed by some great saint's mouth, laid afterwards
With taper flame in middle altar-work,
All over soft as your own lips that fed
Between the king's eyes —
  Ros.   Madam, be merciful,
You hurt me, pinching in my throat so hard.
Alas, ah God, will not one speak for me ?
  Qu. El. Yea, then choose this.
  Ros.   I will not choose ; God help

I will not choose; I have no eyes to choose;
I will be blind and save the sight of choice.
So shall my death, not looking on itself,
Fall like a chance.

    Qu. El.   Put me not past mine oath;
I am sworn deep to lay no stroke on you.

    Ros. I will not drink; so shall I make defeat
On death's own bitter will. Do not look hard;
I know you are more sweet at heart than so.
Make me the servant of your meanest house,
And let your girls smite me some thrice a day,
I will bear that; yea, I will serve and be
Stricken for wage and bruised; give me two days
A poor man puts away for idleness,
Lest my soul ache with you, — nay, but, sweet God,
Is there no thing will say a word for me,
A little sad word said inside her ears
To make them burn for piteous shame? you see
How I weep, yea, fear wrings my body round;
You know not hardly how afraid I am,
But my throat sickens with pure·fear, my blood
Falls marred in me; and God should love you so
Being found his friend and made compassionate —

    Qu. El. I have a mind to pluck thee with my hands,
Tear thy hair backward, tread on thee. By God,
I thought no sin so sick and lame a fool
As this lust is.

    Ros.   But I will drink indeed,

I will not yet ; give me the sword to see
How that must hurt.

    Qu. El.   Yea, this way will you see ?

    Ros. I cannot hold it by the edge ; it is
Too keen to touch the sides thereof with sight.
Yea then, your drink.

    Qu. El.   To spill here in the ground ?
It were good game to get white iron out
As did God's priest with a king's harlot once,
Burn up your hair and brand between your eyes
That I might have you wear me so in red.
Besides to-night the king will look for you,
" Eh, Rosamond ? she hides then closer yet,
May be for fear of passengers that slip
Between those waters ; I shall have her now,
Ha love, have I said right ? " would he kiss you,
Spoilt face and all ? — You will die simply then ?
You do the wiselier.

    Ros.   God be pitiful !
No man in this sharp world to speak for me
Of all that go and talk, — why now they laugh,
Chatter of me, base people, say foul things, —
Ah God, sweet lord, that death should be so hard.
Nay, thou fair death, make me not wroth with thee ;
Use me the best way found in thee, fair death,
And thou shalt have a pleasure of mine end,
For I will kiss thee with a patient lip
Even on this husk of thine ; thou tender death,

Do me none evil and no shame, that am
So soft and have such sufferance of thee
And talk such lovers' little talk ; fair death,
Where thou hast kissed the latest lip of man's
None shall drink after.

Qu. El.   Cease, and be not lewd ;
Cease, and make haste.   What harlot's wit hast thou
To play death's friend this way ?

Ros.   Yea, friends we are ;
I have no breath that makes a curse for you,
All goes to fashion prayer that God sow pity
I' the grounds of wrath ; you see me that I drink ;
So God have patience.

Qu. El.   It is done indeed.
Perchance now it should please you to be sure
This were no poison ? as it is, it is.
Ha, the lips tighten so across the teeth
They should bite in, show blood ; how white she is,
Yea, white ! dead green now like a fingered leaf.

Enter KING HENRY *and* BOUCHARD.

K. Hen. Is it all done ?   Yea, so, love, come to me,
You are quite safe, held fast ; kiss me a little.
Speak, hast thou done ?

Qu. El.   So, would you praise me now ?
It is done well, and as I thought of it.

K. Hen. O sweetest thing, you do not bleed with her ?
She cannot speak.   By God's own holiness

Each fear put on you shall be as blood wrung
From her most damnéd body.   Do but speak.
This is just fear.   Ay, come close in and weep.
This is your fear?

    Ros.   Nay, but my present death.
Doth fear so ruin all the blood in one
As this spoils mine?   Let me get breath to help;
And yet no matter; I will not speak at all,
I can die without speaking.

    K. Hen. (*to the Queen*).   Listen to this, —
Thou art worse caught than anything in hell, —
To put thy hands upon this body — God,
Curse her for me!   I will not slay thee yet,
But damn thee some fine quiet way — O love,
That I might put thee in my heart indeed
To be wept well! thou shalt be healed of her —
Poor sweet; she hath even touched thee in the neck
Thou art so hurt.   This is not possible
O God, that I could see what thou wilt do
With her when she is damned!   Thou piece of hell,
Is there no way to crawl out of my hate
By saving her? pray God then till I come,
For if my hands had room for thee I would
Hew thy face out of shape. — She will not die.
This heat in her is pure, and the sweet life
With holy color doth assure itself
In death's sharp face; she will not die at all.
Thou art all foiled, found fool and laughable

And halt and spat upon and sick, — O love
Make me not mad! if you do so with me
I am but dead.

Ros.　　　　Do not so cry on me;
I am hurt sore, but shall not die of it.
Be gracious with me, set your face to mine,
Tell me sweet things.　I have no pain at all,
I am but woman and make words of pain
Where I am well indeed; only the breath
Catches, for joy to have you close.　I would
Sing your song through; yea, I am good you said,
Gracious and good; I cannot sing that out,
But am I good that kiss your lips or no?
That keeps yet sweet; there is not so much pain
As one might weep for; a little makes us weep;
To die grown old were sad, but I die worth
Being kissed of you; leave me some space to breathe, —
I have thanks yet.　　　　　　　·　　[*Dies.*

Qu. El.　　　　So is the whole played out;
Yea, kiss him.　Ah, my Bouchard, you said that?

K. Hen.　Ay, keep the mouth at ease; shut down the
　　lids;
You see I am not riotously moved,
But peaceable, all heat gone out of me.
This is some trick, some riddle of a dream,
Have you not known such dreams?　I bid you stand,
Being king and lord, I make you come and go;
But say I bid my love turn and kiss me,

No more obedience? here at sight of her
The heart of rule is broken.   No more obedience?
She hath forgotten this ; were I a man,
Even that would slay me ; I beseech you, sir,
Take no care of me ; I can bid you ; see,
I touch her face ; the lips begin to stir,
Gather up color ; is there sound or speech,
Or pleasant red under the white of death?
She will speak surely ; for dead flesh is gray
And even the goodliest pattern wrought of man
Coldness and change disfigure ; what was red
A new disconsolate color overpaints,
And ever with some ill deformity
The secret riddle and pure sense of flesh
Becomes defeated and the rebel taste
Makes new revolt at it ; I pray take note of me,
Here comes no new thing ; do you not see her face,
How it hath shut up close like any flower,
With scents of sleep and hesitating sweet
I' the heaviest petal of it?   Note her eyes,
They move and alter ; and if I touched her lips
(Which lest she wake I will not) they would be
As red as mine ; yea that pure cheek of hers
Turn redder.
    Qu. El.   Will you speak to him?
    Bouch.   Fair lord —
    K. Hen. Sir, pardon me, I know she is but dead,
She is not as I am ; we have sense and soul ;

Who smites me on the mouth or plucks by the hair,
I know what feels it; stab me with a knife,
I can show blood; and when the eyes turn wet,
There 's witness for me and apparent proof
I am no less than man; though in the test
I show so abject and so base a slave
As grooms may snarl at, and your stabled hound
Find place more worth preferment.   For the queen,
See how strong laughter takes her by the throat
And plucks her lips! her teeth would bite, no doubt,
But she keeps quiet; she should live indeed;
She hath mere motion, and such life in her
Accuses and impeaches the Lord God,
Who wrought so miserably the shapes of man
With such sad cunning.   Lo you, sir, she weeps;
Now see I well how vile a thing it is
To wear the label and the print of life
Being fashioned so unhappily; for we
Share no more sense nor worthier scope of time
Than the live breath that is in swine and apes
As honorable, now she that made us right
In the keen balance and sharp scale of God
Becomes as pasture and gross meat for death,
Whereon the common ravin of his throat
Makes rank invasion.   Time was, I could not speak
But she would praise or chide me; now I talk
All this time out, mere baffled waste, to get
That word of her I find not.   Tell me, sweet,

Have I done wrong to thee? spoken thee ill?
Nay, for scorn hurts me, Rosamond; be wise,
As I am patient; do but bow your face, —
By God she will not! Abide you but awhile
And we shall hear her; for she will not fail.
She will just turn her sweet head quietly
And kiss me peradventure; say no word,
And you shall see her; doubtless she will grow
Sorry to vex me; see now, here are two
She hath made weep, and God would punish her
For hardness, ay though she were thrice as fair,
He would not love her; look, she would fain wake,
It makes her mouth move and her eyelids rise
To feel so near me. — Ay, no wiser yet?
Then will I leave you; may be she will weep
To have her hands made empty of me; yea,
Lend me your hand to cover close her face,
That she may sleep well till we twain be gone;
Cover the mouth up; come each side of me.

THE END.

Cambridge : Stereotyped and Printed by Welch, Bigelow, & Co.

www.ingramcontent.com/pod-product-compliance
Lightning Source LLC
Chambersburg PA
CBHW030106030726
47498CB00007B/2270